Maria Parloa

Practical Cookery

With demonstrations

Maria Parloa

Practical Cookery
With demonstrations

ISBN/EAN: 9783744789134

Printed in Europe, USA, Canada, Australia, Japan

Cover: Foto ©Lupo / pixelio.de

More available books at **www.hansebooks.com**

New-York Tribune.

EXTRA NO. 85.

———•———

PRACTICAL COOKERY,

WITH DEMONSTRATIONS.

BY

MISS MARIA PARLOA.

———•———

NEW YORK: THE TRIBUNE.

1884.

PRICE TWENTY-FIVE CENTS.

INTRODUCTION.

Miss Maria Parloa's lectures on cooking have been deservedly praised in New-York and other cities as the best contribution that has yet been made to the most practical of home arts. Her familiar talks to her classes, reduced to writing for the benefit of TRIBUNE readers and carefully revised in print by her own hand, are here reproduced. American house-keepers will find these suggestions and recipes of invaluable assistance not only in provid-ing luxuries, but even necessities, for those who gather at their tables. Miss Parloa is a most practical as well as accomplished woman and is not wanting in originality. These recipes are not adaptations of foreign formulas, but are designed to form a common-sense manual for American kitchens.

CONTENTS.

PRACTICAL COOKERY.

A SERIES OF KITCHEN LESSONS, WITH DEMONSTRATIONS,

BY MISS MARIA PARLOA.

I.

PUFF PASTE, ECLAIRS AND OTHER DAINTY DISHES.

The work that is being done in Miss Parloa's Cooking School, at No. 222 East Seventeenth-st., is exciting increased interest both among the pupils of the school and among many others who have watched its progress. The number of attendants has grown steadily, and the scope of the school is being gradually broadened. At present the work comprises private classes and public demonstration lessons. The several private classes, which are taught both by Miss Parloa and by her assistant, Mrs. Webb, contain six members each. The instructor gives the recipes for the different dishes to be made and the scholars prepare them under the immediate direction of their teacher. In the demonstration lessons Miss Parloa reads the recipes and prepares the dishes herself, explaining every step in the different processes with the utmost care, and in a manner that never fails to interest her hearers, whether they know anything about methods of cooking or not. These lessons are given on Monday and Tuesday of each week.

In her first lecture Miss Parloa treated of the making and uses of puff paste, and this subject drew the largest audience of the season. After prefacing her work with the statement that the hands should first be washed with soap and water, and then dipped in extremely hot, and subsequently in cold, water, Miss Parloa brought to her table a quart of pastry flour, a pint of butter, a tablespoonful of salt, a like quantity of sugar, and one and a quarter cupfuls of ice-water, and said:

"Fill a large pan or bowl with boiling water, and a moment later substitute cold water, leaving the bowl finally only half full. Wash the pint of butter in this water, and work with the hands until light and waxy; this action freeing it of buttermilk and salt and lightening it, so that the pastry will be more delicate. After having shaped the butter into two thin cakes, put it in a pan of ice water to harden. Mix the flour, sugar and salt together, and with the hands rub a third of the butter into the flour. Add the water, stirring with a knife; and continue stirring quickly and vigorously until the paste becomes a smooth ball. Sprinkle the moulding-board *lightly* with flour. Turn the paste on the board and pound it quickly and lightly with the rolling-pin. Be careful not to break the paste. Roll from you and to one side; or, if you prefer to roll from you all the while, turn the paste around. When it has been rolled down to the thickness of about a quarter of an inch, wipe the remaining butter, break it into bits and spread these on the paste. A light sprinkling of flour should follow, and the paste should be folded, one-third from each side, so that the edges meet. Next fold from the ends, but do not have these meet. Double the paste, pound lightly, and roll down to the thickness of about a third of an inch. Fold as before and roll down again. Repeat the operation three times if for pies and six if for *vol-au-vents*, patties or tarts. When it has been rolled for the last time place upon ice. It should remain at least an hour in the ice-chest before it is used. In hot weather if the paste sticks when being rolled, put it on a tin sheet and on ice. As soon as it has been chilled it will roll easily. The smaller the quantity of flour used when rolling the better the paste will be; indeed, no matter how carefully all the work is done, the paste will not be good if much flour be used."

Having had her paste chilled, Miss Parloa made a *vol-au-vent* in this manner: The paste was rolled into a ten-inch square, placed on a plate 9½ inches in diameter and cut around the edge of the plate. Another plate, about 7 inches in diameter, was placed in the centre of the paste, and then a case-knife, that had been dipped into hot water, was used to cut two-thirds through the paste around the edge of the small plate. The paste was put in a flat baking-pan and into the oven. In about a quarter of an hour the draughts were closed, to slacken the heat, and the *vol-au-vent* was cooked about half an hour longer, Miss Parloa being careful that it should not burn. When it was removed from the oven the case-knife was used to lift the centre-piece, and the uncooked paste was removed from the *vol-au-vent* with a spoon. Then the centre-piece was replaced. Miss Parloa explained that at the time for serving, the *vol-au-vent* should be heated through, filled with chicken, sweetbreads, lobster, oysters or something else, and after the cover had been replaced, should be served hot. All the work except this last part could be done the previous day if more convenient.

For patties Miss Parloa rolled a quantity of puff paste down to the thickness of three-quarters of an inch, taking pains to have the thickness even. Pieces were then cut out with a round tin cutter three and a half inches in diameter and placed in pans. Another cutter, two and a half inches in diameter, was dipped into hot water and placed in the centre of each patty, to be pressed about two-thirds through, the motion of pressing being rotary. These centre-pieces, Miss Parloa said, were easily separated from the rest of the patties when baked. The patties were baked ten minutes in a very hot oven, then the heat was reduced, and they were kept in the oven twenty minutes longer. When they were removed the centre-pieces were lifted and the uncooked paste taken out, leaving space for meat or fish chopped fine, seasoned with pepper and salt, and warmed in a cream sauce; the covers being finally replaced.

Spanish curls were next made. The trimmings of puff paste were rolled very thin and cut into long, narrow strips. These were wound around small conical sticks and baked a quarter of an hour. The removal of the sticks gave a place for preserved strawberries and whipped cream.

This was the rule furnished for *gâteau Chantilly:* After rolling puff paste very thin, place a plate upon it and trim the edges with a sharp knife on a jagging-iron. Place the paste on a tin sheet and bake fifteen or twenty minutes in a quick oven. It takes two pastry cakes for the *gâteau.* Put half a pint of rich cream into a bowl with one tablespoonful of sugar and two of wine, and whip to a stiff froth. Cover one side of each of the cakes with strawberry preserve. Place a cake on a plate, the spread side up, and heap whipped cream upon it. Place the other cake upon the first, the covered side down. Sprinkle sugar over the cakes or heap whipped cream upon them and serve—a delicious dish for dessert.

From *gâteau Chantilly* Miss Parloa turned to the filling for the *vol-au-vent,* which she made as follows: Boil a quart of oysters in their own liquor. As soon as scum arises, skim it off. Drain the oysters and return half a pint of the liquor to the saucepan. Mix a scant tablespoonful of flour with two heaping tablespoonfuls of butter, and when the mixture is light and creamy, gradually turn upon it the boiling oyster liquor. Season well with salt

and pepper and possibly with a bare suggestion of nutmeg or mace. After boiling up once, add three tablespoonfuls of cream and also the oysters. Stir over the fire half a minute; then fill the *vol-au-vent* and serve immediately.

Miss Parloa impressed upon her hearers the importance of using "old-process" flour for puff paste, and also the need of working the butter properly and attending carefully to the baking. At the close of the lecture the dishes made during the morning were served to the audience.

On the next afternoon Miss Parloa opened her lecture by giving these recipes for éclairs: Put a cupful of boiling water and half a cupful of butter into a large sauce-pan, and when the mixture boils up turn in a pint of flour. Beat well with a vegetable masher, and when it is perfectly smooth and velvety to the touch remove from the fire. Break five eggs into a bowl, and when the paste is nearly cold beat the eggs into it with the hand. Only a small part of the broken eggs should be added at one time. When the mixture has been thoroughly beaten, say in twenty minutes, spread on buttered sheets in oblong pieces about four inches long and one and a half wide. These pieces must be laid about two inches apart, and must be baked in a rather quick oven for about twenty-five minutes. As soon as they are baked, ice with chocolate or vanilla icing, and when this is cold, cut the éclairs—split them—on one side, and fill.

CHOCOLATE ECLAIRS.—Put a cupful and a half of milk in a double boiler. Beat together two-thirds of a cupful of sugar, two eggs, one-fourth of a cupful of flour and one-fourth of a teaspoonful of salt, and stir this mixture into the boiling milk. Cook fifteen minutes, stirring frequently. When cold, flavor with a teaspoonful of vanilla extract. Put two squares of scraped chocolate with five tablespoonfuls of powdered sugar and three of boiling water, and stir over the fire till smooth and glossy. Dip the tops of the éclairs into this coating as they come from the oven. When the chocolate icing is dry, cut open the éclairs from the side and fill with cold cream. If a chocolate flavor be desired with the cream, add a tablespoonful of dissolved chocolate.

VANILLA ECLAIRS.—Make an icing with the whites of two eggs and a cupful and a half of powdered sugar. Flavor with a teaspoonful of vanilla extract. Frost the éclairs, and, when they are dry, open and fill them. They may be filled with cream, sweetened, flavored with vanilla, and whipped to a stiff froth.

FROSTING —The white of an egg, one teacupful of powdered sugar, a tablespoonful of lemon juice. Put the white into a bowl and add sugar gradually, beating with a spoon. When all has been added stir in the lemon juice. If the white of the egg be large it will require a goodly cupful of sugar, and if it be small a scant cupful will suffice. The egg must *not* be beaten until the sugar has been added. This recipe gives a smooth, tender frosting. The same amount of material, prepared with the whites of the eggs unbeaten, will make one-third less frosting than it will if the eggs be beaten to a stiff froth before the sugar is added, but the frosting will be enough smoother and softer to pay for the use of additional material. Half a teaspoonful of vanilla extract may be used for a flavor.

CREAM CAKES.—Make a mixture like that for éclairs, and drop in spoonfuls upon buttered tins, so that the cakes may be round instead of oblong. The cakes should be allowed to bake with a rough surface and should be filled with a mixture like that for chocolate éclairs.

After the éclairs and cream cakes came queen fritters, for which a paste like that for éclairs was used. This paste was dropped by tablespoonfuls into boiling lard, and cooked until the fritters cracked open. Wine and sugar were the accompaniments when the fritters were served, though sugar alone may be used.

The chief dish of the afternoon was the *gâteau St. Honoré*. This also demanded a paste like éclairs. Miss Parloa said to butter three pie plates, and after rolling puff or chopped paste very thin, to cover the plates with it. She then cut off the paste about an inch from the edge all round the plates and spread a thin layer of the cooked paste over the puff paste. A tube about half an inch in diameter was put into what is called a pastry bag and the remainder of the éclair paste was turned into the bag and pressed through the tube on to the edges of the plate, where the puff paste had been cut off. Care was taken to have the border of even thickness all round. Holes were pricked with a fork in the paste in the centre of the plates, and then the dishes were put in a moderate oven for half an hour. The remaining paste was made into balls the size of common marbles—three dozen. These were dropped into a pan that had been buttered lightly, and were baked fifteen or twenty minutes. While they were baking, half a cupful of water and half a cupful of sugar were put into a small saucepan to boil for twenty-five minutes. When the little balls and the paste in the plates had been cooked, the balls were taken up on the tip of a skewer, dipped into the syrup, which made them adhesive, and placed on the border of paste, about two inches apart. Miss Parloa cautioned her auditors never to stir the syrup, else it would become grained and worthless. A good plan is to pour part of the syrup into a small cup and place the cup in hot water. That which remains in the saucepan should be kept hot—without boiling—until needed. When all the balls had been used, four dozen French candied cherries were dipped into the syrup and placed between the balls. About fifteen cherries were reserved to garnish the centre of the dish. The remaining part of the recipe was as follows: Whip a pint and a half of cream to a froth. Soak half a package of gelatine in half a cupful of milk for two hours. Pour upon this composition half a cupful of boiling milk. Place the pan of whipped cream in another of ice water and sprinkle over it

two-thirds of a cupful of sugar and nearly a teaspoonful of vanilla flavor. Strain the gelatine upon this preparation and stir gently from the bottom until a thickening is perceptible. When it will just pour, fill the three plates with it and set them in the ice-chest for half an hour. Garnish the top with the remaining cherries.

II.

CROQUETTES, OMELETS, BEEFSTEAK, DISHES FOR DESSERT, ETC.

At her school of cookery Miss Parloa began her second lecture with a talk about chicken croquettes. For these she said that there would be needed a solid pint of finely chopped cooked chicken, a cupful of cream or of chicken stock, four eggs, a tablespoonful of salt, half a teaspoonful of pepper, a tablespoonful of flour, a tablespoonful of lemon juice, three tablespoonfuls of butter, one teaspoonful of onion juice and a pint of crumbs. She explained that the onion juice was obtained by peeling the onion and grating on a large grater, using considerable pressure. First, the cream was put on to boil. The butter and flour were soon mixed together and stirred into the boiling stock, and the chicken and seasoning were added. Two minutes later two of the eggs, well beaten, also were added. The dish was then taken from the stove and set away to cool. When the mixture was cold a spoonful was shaped with both hands into the form of a cylinder. The most delicate handling was required, for pressure forces the particles apart and destroys the shape. The croquettes were placed, one by one, on a deep plate containing two beaten eggs, slightly thick, and several spoonfuls of the egg were poured over each croquette. When they had been well covered they were removed—a case-knife being slipped under them—to a board covered thickly with crumbs, on which they were rolled until wholly crumbed. They were next placed in a frying-basket, a few at a time, so they should not touch each other, and plunged into boiling fat. In about a minute and a half they had turned to a rich brown, and were laid on brown paper in a warm pan.

The next topic—a seasonable one—was "Omelets."
"It is a pity," said Miss Parloa, "that more people do not realize how appetizing eggs are in this form and how easy it is to make a good omelet. A large proportion of the failures are due to an omission to have the pan hot enough, or to the use of too many eggs at one time. When too much beaten egg is used, part will be cooked hard before the rest is heated through. For four eggs a pan with a diameter of eight inches is large enough; if more eggs be used, a larger pan will be needed."

A plain omelet was made of four eggs, two tablespoonfuls of milk, one tablespoonful of butter and a teaspoonful of salt. The eggs were beaten and the salt and milk added. In the meantime the omelet-pan had been on the stove, and had become very hot. A spoonful of butter was dropped into it and quickly melted. Immediately the beaten eggs were poured in, and the pan was shaken vigorously on the hottest part of the stove (somewhat as a corn-popper is shaken) until the egg had begun to thicken. A few seconds later it gradually browned. A knife was run between the edge of the omelet and the sides of the pan and the omelet was folded and turned out on a hot dish, to be eaten at once.

A cheese omelet was made in much the same way; three tablespoonfuls of grated cheese being sprinkled upon the eggs when they began to thicken. For a chicken omelet a cupful of cooked chicken, cut rather fine and warmed in cream sauce, was substituted for cheese. This sauce was made of a pint of cream, a generous tablespoonful of flour, and salt and pepper to taste. The cream was allowed to reach the boiling point. Half a cupful was reserved, however, and mixed with the flour until smooth. Then this mixture was stirred into the boiling cream; the seasoning was added, and after three minutes' boiling the sauce was finished. For a savory omelet a little salt and a tablespoonful of chopped parsley were added to the mixture for a plain omelet, and it was stated that a little grated onion might be used, too. A jelly omelet was made like the other, currant jelly being spread upon the egg just before it was folded. Miss Parloa reminded her audience that an omelet should never be made until wanted, as it is not at all toothsome if allowed to stand after coming from the stove.

For crême à la Versailles, Miss Parloa said: " Put half a cupful of sugar in a small frying-pan and stir until it is a very light brown. Add two tablespoonfuls of water, and after stirring a moment longer, mix with the milk. Beat together with a spoon seven eggs and half a teaspoonful of salt; then add to the mixture of sugar, water and milk, and add half a teaspoonful of vanilla flavor at the same time. After buttering lightly a two-quart charlotte-russe mould, put the custard in it. Put the mould in a basin of warm (not hot) water and bake slowly until the custard is firm in the centre. It should take forty minutes; but if the oven be quite hot, the custard will bake in half an hour, 'Test it by thrusting a knife down in the centre; for if the custard be not milky, it is done. Set away in a cold place until serving time. The cream should be ice cold when eaten. Turn out on a flat dish and pour caramel sauce over it. Caramel sauce is made by putting a cupful of sugar in a small frying-pan and stirring over the fire until a dark brown if you like a strong flavor or till a light brown if you prefer a delicate flavor; adding a cupful of boiling water and simmering fifteen minutes. The same should be set away to cool."

For cheese soufflé Miss Parloa used a heaping tablespoonful of flour, three eggs, a cupful of grated cheese, half a cupful of milk, two tablespoonfuls of butter, half a teaspoonful of salt, a "speck" of cayenne. The butter was put in a saucepan, and when it was hot the flour was added and stirred until smooth but not browned. Then the milk and

seasoning were added, and after two minutes' cooking the yolks of the eggs, well beaten, and the cheese were added. The mixture was set away, and when it became cold the whites, beaten to a stiff froth, were added. The soufflé was turned into a buttered escalloped dish, holding about a quart, and baked from twenty to twenty-five minutes. It was served as soon as it came from the oven.

Miss Parloa opened her lecture the next afternoon with a dissertation on beefsteak. "Never be satisfied to have it cut less than three-quarters of an inch thick if you wish it rich, and do not pound the juice out of it. Trim off any suet that has been left on by the butcher and dredge the meat with salt, pepper and flour. A double broiler is the best utensil for cooking it. The steak should be kept over or before clear coals for ten minutes if to be rare, or twelve if to be rather well done. It should be turned constantly; but never thrust a knife or fork into it to see how it is cooking. Serve on a hot dish with maître d'hôtel butter, which is made of four tablespoonfuls of butter, one of lemon juice, one of vinegar, a teaspoonful of chopped parsley, half a teaspoonful of salt and a quarter of a teaspoonful of pepper; the butter being beaten to a cream, and the other ingredients gradually beaten into it. The sauce is to be spread on the steak."

Attention was next given to the making of a Nesselrode pudding. This required a pint can of pineapple, a pint of cream, the yolks of ten eggs, a pint of shelled almonds, a pint and a half of shelled chestnuts, half a pound of French candied fruit, a pint of water, a pint of sugar, four tablespoonfuls of wine, one tablespoonful of vanilla flavor, half a teaspoonful of salt. After the chestnuts had boiled for half an hour the black skins were rubbed off and the meats were pounded in a mortar until they become a paste. The almonds were blanched (placed for a moment in boiling, and then in cold, water and rubbed between the hands) and treated like the chestnuts. The juice from the pineapple and the sugar and water were boiled for twenty minutes in a saucepan; and the yolks of the eggs were beaten, and stirred into the syrup. The saucepan was placed in another containing boiling water and the mixture was beaten with an eggbeater until it began to thicken. It was then placed in a basin of cold water and beaten ten minutes longer. The chestnuts and almonds were mixed with the cream and rubbed through a sieve. To them were added the candied fruit and the pineapple, cut fine, and this mixture was put with that in the saucepan. The flavors and salt were added, and the pudding was frozen like ice-cream.

Miss Parloa announced the ingredients for angel cake to be the whites of eleven eggs, one cupful of pastry flour, measured after it has been sifted four times; one and a half cupfuls of granulated sugar, a teaspoonful of vanilla flavor and a like quantity of cream of tartar. She said to sift the flour and cream of tartar together. Beat the egg whites to a stiff froth, and beat in the sugar; after which add the flavor and flour, stirring quickly and lightly.

Beat until ready to put the mixture into the oven. Use a pan (made for the purpose) that has little legs at the top corners, so that when the pan is turned upside down on the table, after the baking, a current of air will pass under as well as over the cake. Do not grease the pan. Bake for forty minutes in a moderate oven. Miss Parloa told her hearers that several points must be carefully observed: There is no soda used; the eggs must be beaten to a stiff froth; the sugar should be beaten into the eggs gradually; the cake must bake slowly.

Scallops were prepared in two ways: First, they were drained, seasoned with pepper and salt, and dipped in beaten egg and then in bread crumbs. They were put in a frying-basket and plunged into boiling fat, being cooked a minute and a half. After they had stood a while on brown paper they were served on a hot dish with a garnish of parsley and slices of lemon.

For creamed scallops Miss Parloa took a quart of the fish, a pint of milk, a tablespoonful of flour, two tablespoonfuls of butter, and salt and pepper. The milk was put in the double boiler, and while the scallops were being drained, the butter and flour were beaten together until creamy. This mixture, together with the seasoning, was stirred into the boiling milk, and the scallops were cooked seven minutes.

III.

FILLET OF BEEF, CARAMEL ICE CREAM CAKES, ETC.

Miss Parloa began the lesson by cutting the tenderloin from a sirloin roast, or what is commonly called in New-York a porterhouse roast. The piece weighed about fourteen pounds. When the tenderloin had been removed the flank also was cut off. It was stated that the fillet—the tenderloin—costs $1 a pound, and that if a fillet be wanted it is advisable to buy a large roasting piece and obtain the fillet in that way. The flank may be stuffed and rolled, or is good for stewing or braising; the roast serving for a meal some other day.

With these introductory remarks Miss Parloa, using a sharp knife, removed every shred of muscle, ligament and thin, tough skin from the fillet, which she then skewered into good shape. With the knife she drew a line through the centre of the piece, and she began larding, having two rows of pork, inserted in the two sides of the fillet, meet at the line she had drawn. For the operation a larding needle was, of course, used. The strips of pork were about three inches long and as large round as a lead pencil; they had been kept some time in a bowl of ice to harden. The fillet was well dredged with pepper, salt and flour and put, without water, in a very small pan. For half an hour it was kept in a hot oven. It was stated that on account of the shape of fillets half an hour cooks one weighing either two or six pounds.

Hollandaise or tomato sauce, or potato balls, might

properly have been served with the fillet, but Miss Parloa chose white mushroom sauce instead, using in its preparation a can of French mushrooms, a cupful of white stock, a cupful of cream, three heaping tablespoonfuls of flour, four of butter, salt and pepper to taste. When the butter had been melted the flour was added, the mixture being cooked until smooth, but not brown. Gradually the stock was added, and when it boiled up, the liquor from the mushrooms was put in; followed after five minutes' cooking by the mushrooms, cream and salt and pepper. The sauce was allowed to boil up once and was then poured around the fillet.

Rolled flank of beef was next on the programme. The flank weighed above five pounds. It was carefully wiped with a damp cloth and dredged with salt and pepper. When it lay upon the table one part was seen to be thicker than the other, and some of the meat was cut from the thick portion and laid upon the thin. A dressing was made of a cupful of cracker crumbs, a teaspoonful of summer savory, a tablespoonful of butter, quantities of salt and pepper, and cold water enough to make the cracker quite moist. The meat, having been spread with this dressing, was rolled up, tied and pinned in a cloth. It was placed in a stewpan and just covered with boiling water; and when this water had again reached the boiling point the pan was set back where the water would only bubble. There the meat stood until near the close of the lesson. It was finally allowed to cool in the water in which it was boiled. When nearly cold it was taken up and the cloth was removed, but not the strings. When wholly cold the flank was cut into tender round slices. It was stated that the water could be used as a foundation for a vegetable, rice or tomato soup, or, thickened with flour, could be used as a gravy.

A cupful of water, a cupful of granulated sugar and the juice of a lemon were boiled together for half an hour. Miss Parloa dipped the point of a skewer into the syrup and then into water, and finding that the thread thus formed broke off brittle, announced that the syrup was ready for use on fruit. She pared some oranges, divided them into eighths, and wiped the parts free of moisture. Part of the syrup was poured into a small cup, which was set in a basin of boiling water. The pieces of orange were taken up separately on the point of a skewer and dipped into the syrup, and were afterward placed on a dish that had been buttered lightly. This gave *fruit glacé.* Grapes and nuts were prepared the same way. Special pains were taken to avoid stirring the syrup, for stirring would have spoiled it.

Before making caramel ice cream Miss Parloa said that the foundation she was about to prepare was suitable for all kinds of ice-cream. Having heated a generous pint of milk to the boiling point, she stirred into it a cupful of sugar, a scant half cupful of flour and two eggs, all beaten together; and the mixture was allowed to cook twenty minutes longer, receiving a frequent stirring. A small cupful of sugar was next put in a small frying-pan and stirred over the fire until it turned liquid and began to smoke. It was then turned into the boiling mixture or foundation, when was at once put away to cool. When it became cool a quart of cream was added. Miss Parloa said the flavor of the ice-cream could be varied by browning the sugar more or less.

The mixture was strained into a freezer and directions for packing were given. The ice was broken into pieces about as big as a pint bowl and then put into a canvas bag and pounded with a mallet until the pieces were as small as a hen's egg, or even smaller. After the can containing the cream had been properly adjusted in the freezer, a layer of ice five inches deep was packed around it. A liberal sprinkling of rock salt on the ice was the next act. Alternate layers of ice and salt were continued until the tub was full; the packing being pounded with a paddle. The crank of the freezer being turned a few times, caused the ice to settle somewhat, and more was added. For Miss Parloa said that if the packing be solid at first there need be no repacking. She laid especial stress on the fact that the water must not be drawn off. It fills all the crevices and gives the can a complete cold envelope. For a gallon freezer about ten quarts of ice and three pints of salt are required. With more salt it would take less time for freezing, but the cream would not be so smooth. At first the crank should not be turned very fast, but the speed should be increased as the work becomes harder.

When the cream was finally frozen—as indicated by the extreme difficulty with which the crank was turned—Miss Parloa carefully wiped the salt and ice from the cover of the can and removed the cover without displacing the can itself. The beater was removed and the cream scraped from it, and a large spoon was worked up and down in the can until the cream was light and the space left vacant by the removal of the beater was filled. The cover of the can was replaced, a cork was put in the hole from which the handle of the beater was taken, and the freezer was set aside for a while. When she came to serve the cream, Miss Parloa placed the can for a few seconds in a pan of warm water so that the heat caused the cream to slip out easily upon a dish. She said that if cream is to be moulded it should be removed from the can when the beater is removed; and when it is put into the mould it should be worked up and down with a spoon, so that it shall be tightened, and worked into every part of the mould as well. A sheet of white paper should be placed over the cream before the cover of the mould is put on and the mould should be buried in fresh ice and salt.

A delicious soup, tapioca cream, was the first dish prepared at the usual afternoon lecture, and in its manufacture were used a quart of white stock, a pint of cream, two stalks of celery, an onion a third of a cupful of tapioca, two cupfuls of cold water, a tablespoonful of butter, a small piece of mace, and small quantities of salt and pepper. The tapioca had been washed in advance and soaked over night. It was cooked very gently for an hour, together with the stock. The onion and celery were cut into small pieces and put on to cook for twenty minutes with the mace and milk, and then the contents of this second dish were strained upon the tapioca and stock. The butter, salt and pepper were added, and the soup served at once.

Soda biscuit were made of a quart of unsifted flour, a tablespoonful of sugar, a tablespoonful of butter, three teaspoonfuls of baking powder, one teaspoonful of salt, and milk enough (nearly a pint) to make a soft dough. Lard or drippings might have been used instead of butter, and water instead of milk. The dry ingredients were mixed together and rubbed through a sieve; then the milk was added, and the mixture stirred with a spoon until a smooth paste had been formed. The moulding-board having been sprinkled lightly with flour, the dough was rolled down to the thickness of about half an inch. It was cut into small cakes, and these were baked fifteen minutes in a *very* hot oven.

Fairy gingerbread was made of two cupfuls of sugar, four of flour, one of milk, one of butter, a tablespoonful of ginger and three-fourths of a teaspoonful of soda. When the butter had been beaten to a cream the sugar was gradually added, followed, when the mixture became light, by the ginger, the milk (in which the soda had been allowed in the meantime to dissolve), and finally the flour. Baking pans were turned upside down, the bottoms were wiped clean and then buttered, and the cake mixture was spread upon them very thin. The gingerbread was baked in a moderate oven until brown, and, while still *hot*, it was cut into squares with a case-knife and slipped off of the pan. Miss Parloa said that the two important points to be remembered are, to spread the mixture thin as a wafer and cut it the instant it is taken from the oven. The gingerbread should be kept in a tin box. A large dish can be made with the quantities of ingredients given above.

For Ames cake there were used three cupfuls of pastry flour, two of sugar, a generous cupful of butter, a small cupful of milk, the yolks of five eggs and the whites of three, a teaspoonful of cream of tartar, half a teaspoonful of soda, one teaspoonful of lemon extract. Miss Parloa said that a spoonful and a half of baking powder might be substituted for the cream of tartar and soda, and the juice of a fresh lemon for the teaspoonful of the extract. The butter having been beaten to a cream, the sugar was added gradually, then the flavor, the eggs (well beaten), the milk, and finally the flour, with the soda and cream of tartar mixed with it. The whole mixture was stirred quickly and thoroughly, and baked in two sheets in a moderate oven for twenty-five or thirty minutes. The loaves were covered with a frosting made by stirring two small cupfuls of powdered sugar into the whites of two eggs, seasoning with lemon.

Part of the Ames cake was cut into small squares, and after a small portion of the crust had been removed from each, the cavities were filled with preserved strawberries. The pieces of crust were replaced, and the cakes, covered with icing made after a recipe already published, became Vieunois cakes.

Part of the Ames cake also was cut into small oblong pieces, which were frosted on the top and sides. When the frosting had become hard Miss Parloa drew dark lines and made dots with a little brush that she dipped into melted chocolate, giving the cakes the semblance and name of dominos.

IV.

HAM, TONGUE, BAKED BEANS, EGGS, MUFFINS, ETC.

Miss Parloa began her lesson by giving directions for baking beans in the Boston style. A quart of beans had been freed of stones and dirt, washed clean, and soaked over night in cold water. The water was poured off and enough warm water put in to cover the beans. A pound of rather lean salt pork was added, and the dish was allowed to boil moderately for half an hour. The beans were then turned into a colander, and three quarts of cold water were poured over them. Half the beans were put in a bean-pot, then the pork, with its rind scored, and then the rest of the beans, and over them was poured a mixture composed of a teaspoonful of mustard, a tablespoonful of salt, a tablespoonful of molasses and a cupful of water. Enough boiling water to just cover the beans was added, and they were put into a slow oven to cook *slowly* for ten hours. Miss Parloa said that it is this slow cooking, with the occasional addition of a little water so as to keep the beans moist and covered all the time, which makes the dish nice. The use of mustard lessens the liability of distress from eating of the beans. Where pork is not liked, two pounds of corned beef can be substituted. When ready for serving, the beans have a rich brown color and are moist and whole. In this instance the testing of the dish was postponed till the next day, because, as already remarked, many hours were needed for the cooking.

After the disposition of the beans attention was given to the roasting of a ham. The ham weighed ten pounds. Previous to the lesson it had been washed and boiled gently for three hours in just enough water to cover. The skin was removed and the meat was put in a large baking-pan and placed in a moderate oven. When it was taken out it was a rosy brown. Part of it was served to the ladies with champagne sauce, made by this recipe: "Mix thoroughly a tablespoonful of butter with one of flour. Set the saucepan on the fire, and stir constantly until the mixture is dark brown; then pour into it half a pint of boiling gravy (the liquor in which pieces of lean meat have boiled until it is very rich). Pour in this gravy slowly, and stir slowly and continually." After the sauce has boiled up once, season it well with pepper and salt, and strain; then add half a cupful of champagne or wine.

For *eggs brouillé* Miss Parloa cut two mushrooms into dice and fried them for a minute in a tablespoonful of butter. She beat together half-a-dozen eggs, a teaspoonful of salt, a little pepper and half a cupful of cream and put them in a saucepan. The mushrooms and two tablespoonfuls of butter were added to these ingredients, and the mixture was stirred over a moderate fire until it began to thicken. It was then taken from the fire and beaten rapidly until the eggs had become quite thick and creamy. Slices of toast were spread upon a hot platter and the mixture was heaped upon them. A garnish of points of toast—thin slices cut into triangles—was added.

Coddled eggs proved to be a simple but palatable dish. The eggs were put in a warm saucepan and covered with boiling water, and were kept for ten minutes where they remained hot but did not boil. By this method both the whites and yolks were well cooked.

Eggs *sur le plat*, for which dishes are made expressly, were prepared in this way: A little dish was heated and buttered, and two eggs were broken into it, care being taken not to break the yolks. After a sprinkling of salt and pepper, half a teaspoonful of butter, broken into small pieces, was dropped upon the eggs, and the dish was kept in the oven, in a moderate heat, until the whites of the eggs had become "set"—say five minutes. Miss Parloa said a dish should be allowed for each person, and that the flavor might be varied by sprinkling a little finely chopped ham or parsley upon the plate before breaking the eggs.

Still another mode of serving eggs—in cream—was shown. Six eggs were boiled for twenty minutes. From a pint of milk half a cupful was taken and mixed with a generous tablespoonful of flour until it was smooth; and as soon as the remaining milk had been heated to the boiling point this mixture was stirred into it. Pepper and salt were added, and the sauce was boiled for three minutes. Six slices of toast were laid on a hot dish, and upon each was spread a layer of sauce, then part of the whites of the eggs, cut into thin strips, and then part of the yolks, rubbed through a sieve. This operation was repeated, and finally a third layer of sauce was spread. The dish was placed in the oven for three minutes, and was afterward garnished with parsley.

At the usual afternoon lecture a fresh beef tongue was washed, and a trussing needle, with strong twine attached, was run through the roots and end of it, the two parts being drawn together and the twine tied. The tongue was covered with boiling water and boiled gently for two hours, after which it was drained. Six tablespoonfuls of butter were put in a braising-pan, and when the pan was hot, half a small carrot, half a small turnip and two onions, all cut fine, also were put in. They were cooked five minutes, being stirred all the while, and were then drawn to one side. The tongue was rolled in flour and put in the pan, and as soon as it had been browned on one side, it was turned and browned on the other. A quart of the water in which it was boiled was added, as were also a small piece of cinnamon, a clove, a bouquet of sweet herbs (two sprigs of thyme, two bay leaves, two of summer savory, two leaves of sage and two sprigs of parsley tied together), and salt and pepper. The tongue was covered and cooked two hours in a slow oven. It was frequently basted with the gravy in the pan and with salt, pepper and flour. When it had been cooking an hour and a half, the juice of half a lemon was added to the gravy. When the tongue was cooked it was taken up and two spoonfuls of glaze (consommé boiled down) were melted and poured over it. It was then put in a heater while a tablespoonful of cornstarch was mixed with a little cold water and stirred into the boiling gravy, of which there was a pint. This gravy was boiled a moment, strained and poured over the tongue, which was finally garnished with parsley.

After the tongue came an orange pudding, for which these ingredients were used: Six eggs, six large or eight small sweet oranges, a cup and a half of granulated sugar and six tablespoonfuls of the powdered, a quart of milk and half a package of gelatine. The gelatine had been soaked for two hours in a cupful of the milk previous to the lecture. The remaining milk was put into a double boiler, and the yolks of the eggs and the granulated sugar were beaten together. When the milk began to boil the gelatine was stirred into it, and then the beaten yolks and sugar. The mixture was stirred constantly for about five minutes, when it began to thicken, and it was then removed from the stove to a cool place. The oranges were pared, divided into eighths, and freed of seeds and tough parts, and were put into a large glass dish. When the custard had cooled it was poured over them, and the pudding was put in a cool place. (It would have been allowed to remain there six or eight hours if the ladies had not wished to taste it.) The whites of the eggs were beaten to a stiff froth and the powdered sugar gradually added and beaten, and the pudding was covered with this mixture.

Several kinds of muffins were made. The recipes are subjoined:

GRANULATED WHEAT MUFFINS.—Use one and a half cupfuls of fine, granulated wheat (such as is prepared by the Health Food Company), two tablespoonfuls of sugar, one teaspoonful of cream-of-tartar, half a teaspoonful of soda (or one and a half teaspoonfuls of baking powder may be substituted for these last two ingredients), half a teaspoonful of salt, a cupful of milk, one-third of a cupful of water and an egg. Mix the dry ingredients together. Beat the egg till light, add the milk and water to it, and stir into the dry mixture. Bake in buttered muffin-pans in a quick oven for twenty-five minutes. A dozen muffins can be made with the quantities given above. Flour made of

whole wheat by the Franklin Mills can be used instead of granulated wheat.

GRAHAM MUFFINS.—Into a sieve put half a pint of flour, two teaspoonfuls of cream-of-tartar and one of saleratus. Mix the three ingredients thoroughly and sift them into a bowl containing one and a half pints of graham, half a cupful of sugar and a teaspoonful of salt. Mix all thoroughly while dry, and add two well-beaten eggs and a pint of milk. Fill muffin-cups about two-thirds to the top, and bake in a quick oven.

V.

BONED TURKEY, QUINCE ICED PUDDING, AND OTHER DESSERT.

Miss Parloa departed from her custom of preparing a number of dishes, and showed instead how to bone a turkey. Her first remark to her audience was to be careful to obtain a turkey that had not been frozen, because freezing makes the flesh tear easily. She also said to see to it that every part is whole, for a break in the skin would be an insuperable defect. She cut off the legs, at the joints, and the tips of the wings. The bird was not drawn. Placing it on its breast, Miss Parloa, using a sharp boning-knife, cut in a straight line through to the bone, from the neck down to that part of the bird where there is but little flesh—where it is all skin and fat. Beginning at the neck she ran the knife between the meat and bones until she came to the wing, cutting the ligaments that hold the bones together and the tendons that hold the flesh to the bones. With the thumb and forefinger she carefully pressed the meat from the smooth bone; separating the ligaments when she came to the joint and removing the bone. She cautioned her auditors not to try to take out the bone at the next joint, as it gave the turkey a more natural shape and would not be in the way when carving. She next operated near the wishbone, and when it was free from the flesh, ran the knife between the sides and the flesh, always using the fingers to press the meat from the smooth bones, as the breast-bone and lower part of the sides. Miss Parloa worked around the legs the same as around the wings, being exceedingly careful when at the joints not to cut the skin. Drawing the leg-bones out caused that part of the bird to turn inside out. The bird itself was turned over, and the knife was plied skilfully on the other side, the skin being finally drawn from the breast-bone and the knife run between the fat and bone at the rump. The small bone at the extremity was not touched, as it helps to keep the skewers in place. The flesh was slowly removed from the skeleton and turned right side out again.

Some of these directions may appear very complex, but all were clear as given by Miss Parloa while she suited her action to her words. Into the flesh she rubbed a little pepper and two tablespoonfuls of salt, and the whole cavity was then filled with dressing. The back, neck and vent were sewed up, and the turkey was trussed the same as if not boned.

It was next pinned firmly into a strong piece of cotton cloth, which was drawn especially tight at the legs; for this is the broadest part, and unless the precaution be taken, the shape will not be good. Miss Parloa went on to say that the bird would be steamed three hours, and then placed on a buttered tin sheet and put in a baking-pan, and after being basted well with butter, salt, pepper and flour, would be roasted an hour. She said it ought to be basted every ten minutes—twice with stock. When cold, the skewers and strings were to be removed and the turkey garnished with aspic jelly, cooked beets and parsley. In regard to carving, she said to cut off the wings, then two thick slices from the neck, where it will be fat, and then cut thin slices. Jelly should be served on each plate.

The filling used was made of these ingredients: The flesh of a chicken weighing four pounds, half a pound of clear salt pork, a pound of clear veal, a small cupful of cracker crumbs, a cupful of broth, two and a half tablespoonfuls of salt, half a teaspoonful of pepper, the same quantity of sage, a teaspoonful each of thyme, summer savory and sweet marjoram, and, if one likes, a tablespoonful of capers, a quart of oysters and two tablespoonfuls of onion juice (obtained by grating). All the meat was uncooked and there were no tough pieces. It was chopped very fine, and when the other ingredients had been added, all were mixed thoroughly. Miss Parloa remarked that if oysters were used, half the veal must be omitted. She said further that chicken could be substituted for veal, which was recommended simply because of its cheapness.

Aspic jelly was made of a pint and a half of clear stock (beef if for amber jelly, or chicken or veal if for white), half a cupful of cold water, the white of an egg, half a box of gelatine, a large slice of onion, two cloves, a dozen peppercorns, a stalk of celery, salt to taste. The gelatine was soaked in the cold water for two hours; the white of the egg was beaten together with a spoonful of the stock. The ingredients all were then put together and allowed to heat to the boiling point, and were then set back for twenty minutes where they would only simmer. The liquor was strained through a napkin into a mould and put away to harden. Miss Parloa said that aspic jelly can be made by washing the bones of the turkey and chicken, covering them with cold water, and boiling this down to three pints; then straining and setting away to cool, and in the morning skimming off all the fat and turning off the clear stock. But the bones may be used instead for a soup.

Miss Parloa said that although plain roast turkey has a better flavor than boned turkey, the latter is an excellent dish for occasions where it is impracticable to provide any food that cannot be eaten without the use of a knife. A turkey weighing eight or nine pounds before being boned will generally be sufficient for thirty persons at a party; and if the supper be very elaborate, such a turkey may suffice for seventy-five persons.

At the afternoon lesson a number of dishes for dessert were made, among them a quince iced pudding. Three eggs were beaten very light, and when a cupful and a half of sugar had been added the beating was continued until the mixture was foamy. Two cupfuls of sifted pastry flour were put into a sieve and a teaspoonful of cream-of-tartar and half a teaspoonful of soda were added. Half a cupful of cold water was stirred into the beaten eggs and sugar, and the flour was sifted into the same bowl. A double oval mould, tapering, was brought into use at this stage. It was about four inches high, and the measurement at the top, where it opened, was six inches by eight. The space between the outer and inner walls was about an inch and a half. When this mould had been buttered the cake mixture was poured into it, to be baked slowly for forty-five minutes. It was allowed to stand in the mould until nearly cold, and then turned out upon a flat dish. Into the whites of two eggs a cupful and a half of powdered sugar was beaten, seasoned with half a teaspoonful of vanilla extract. The cake was iced with this, and set away to dry. In the meantime a generous quart of cream, a cupful of sugar, a pint of soft custard and a tablespoonful of vanilla flavor were combined and frozen like ice cream. A large tumbler of quince jelly was spread on the inside of the cake, and the frozen cream was put in the centre, while whipped cream was heaped on the top and at the base, making an elegant dish. Miss Parloa said that the cream should not be put into the pudding until just before it was to be served.

Blanc-mange was one of the dishes on the programme. Miss Parloa said it could be made in a variety of ways. In this instance she would use sea-moss farina as the distinctive ingredient. A level tablespoonful was required, and a quart of milk, three tablespoonfuls of sugar, a teaspoonful of vanilla flavor and half a teaspoonful of salt also were used. The milk having been put into a double-boiler, the farina was sprinkled into it. The milk was stirred all the while, and while it was heating it was often stirred. When it boiled up and looked white the sugar, salt and flavor were added; then the mixture was strained, turned into a mould that had been dipped into cold water, and set away to harden. Miss Parloa said it ought to stand for three hours.

For a cottage pudding Miss Parloa softened a spoonful of butter and beat it to a froth, together with a cupful of sugar and two eggs. A cupful of milk was added; also a pint of flour, into which a teaspoonful of soda and two teaspoonfuls of cream-of-tartar had been stirred. The mixture was flavored with lemon and baked in two shallow dishes in a moderate oven for half an hour. It was stated that to the minds of some people it is an improvement to sift sugar over the pudding before baking.

A delicate Indian pudding was easily made. A quart of milk was boiled in a double-boiler, and into it were sprinkled two heaping tablespoonfuls of Indian meal, the milk being stirred all the while. The cooking was continued, with frequent stirring, for twelve minutes. In the meantime three eggs, a teaspoonful of salt, four tablespoonfuls of sugar and half a teaspoonful of ginger were beaten together. A tablespoonful of butter was stirred into the milk and meal, and these ingredients were poured gradually upon the egg mixture. The pudding was baked slowly for an hour.

German pudding sauce was made of three eggs, half a cupful of water, a cupful of sugar, one tablespoonful of butter and three of brandy. A teaspoonful of vanilla extract can be substituted for the liquor. The sugar and water were boiled in a saucepan for a quarter of an hour. The yolks of the eggs were beaten and stirred into this syrup. The saucepan was next put into another basin containing hot water, and the mixture was beaten with a whisk till it began to thicken; then the butter was added, and the brandy and whites of the eggs, beaten to a stiff froth. With a minute's stirring the sauce was finished.

LEMON PIES.—Line two deep tin plates with a paste rolled very thin. Set in a cool place until the filling is made. Beat to a froth three teacupfuls of sugar, the rind and juice of three lemons, and the yolks of six eggs; then beat the whites to a stiff froth and stir into the sugar and other ingredients with three tablespoonfuls of milk. Fill the two plates with this mixture and bake in a moderate oven forty-five minutes. Thorough beating of the mixture and the slow baking are absolutely necessary to the success of the dish.

VI.
ENTREES AND SOUPS.

Previous to her lecture Miss Parloa cleaned a plump chicken and put it on to boil, allowing a pint of water for each pound of the chicken's weight. When the water had been heated to the boiling point it was carefully skimmed, and the kettle was set back where the meat would simmer until very tender—say for an hour and a half. The chicken was then skinned, and after the flesh had been removed from the bones the latter were put back into the kettle to boil until the liquor had been reduced one-half. The liquor was strained and set away to cool during the night.

At the opening of the lecture on this day the fat was skimmed from this hardened liquor and the jelly remaining was turned into a clean saucepan, Miss Parloa being watchful that no sediment followed. Saying that for each quart of the jelly there should now be used a quarter of a package of gelatine (soaked for an hour in half a cupful of cold water), twelve peppercorns, four cloves, a small piece of mace, a stalk of celery, an onion, the white and shell of an egg, and salt and pepper to taste, Miss Parloa added the proper quantities, and after letting the ingredients boil up once, she set the saucepan back where they would simmer for twenty minutes. The jelly was then strained through a napkin. A layer of it, three-quarters of an inch thick, was put into a three-pint mould and into ice-water to harden. The flesh of the chicken was cut into long, thin strips, which were seasoned

well with salt and pepper and laid lightly in the mould when the jelly had become hard. Cool liquid jelly was poured over the meat and was hardened by means of cold. When the dish was ready for serving the mould was dipped into warm water and turned upside down on a platter, its contents sliding out in one mass. A garnish of parsley improved its appearance; and it was stated that Tartar or mayonnaise sauce also might be added.

The next entrée prepared was lambs' tongue in jelly. Three tongues, having been boiled until tender (about two hours), were skinned, and their roots were trimmed off. A quart and half a pint of aspic jelly in liquid state was at hand, and enough was poured into a two quart mould to cover the bottom an inch deep. It was allowed to harden, and in the meantime leaves were cut out of cooked beets with a fancy vegetable cutter. They were carefully laid upon the jelly in the mould, as a garnish, and liquid jelly—perhaps three tablespoonfuls—was gently poured in to hold the leaves in place. When this jelly was solid, enough more was poured in to cover the pieces of beet, and it was allowed to become very hard. Then the tongues were put in, together with half a cupful of jelly, to hold them in place. Some time later the remaining jelly was added, and the dish was put where it would become solid. It was served like the chicken in jelly, only the garnish on the platter consisted of pickled beets as well as parsley.

A white fricassée of chicken next engaged the attention of the class. A chicken weighing about four pounds was boiled until tender. The meat was freed of skin and fat and cut into handsome pieces. Three tablespoonfuls of butter was put into a frying-pan, and when hot it was joined by two tablespoonfuls of flour. The mixture was stirred until smooth and frothy, and there was gradually added a pint of the liquor in which the chicken had boiled. After five minutes' simmering, salt and pepper were added. The chicken also was seasoned, and was then heated in this sauce for about eight minutes, when half a cupful of milk or cream was added. The dish required no further cooking than to boil up once. A mound of mashed and browned potato was put upon a platter and the chicken was disposed around it; a garnish of parsley being finally added.

Soups were next in order. The first was mock bisque. Three pints of milk—less half a cupful—were put into a double kettle to boil, and a quart of canned tomato was put on to stew. The milk reserved was mixed smoothly with a large tablespoonful of flour, and this paste was at once stirred into the boiling milk, which was to cook ten minutes. A large tablespoonful of soda was added to the tomato, which was stirred well at this point and was afterward rubbed through a strainer fine enough to retain the seeds. A piece of butter the size of an egg and proper quantities of salt and pepper were added to the boiling milk, and finally the tomato was added. Miss Parloa said that it only half the quantities were used throughout, the tomato should be stirred well before it is taken from the can, because the liquid portion is more acid than the solid.

For tomato soup a quart of canned tomatoes and a pint of hot water were heated to the boiling point, and into them were stirred two heaping spoonfuls of flour, one of butter and one of tomato, mixed together. A teaspoonful each of salt and sugar was added, and after boiling for a quarter of an hour the soup was rubbed through a sieve. With it were served little squares of toasted bread—the bread having been cut into thin slices, buttered, cut into squares, and browned in a quick oven, buttered side up.

Miss Parloa omitted her usual afternoon lecture and gave a talk on "Marketing" instead.

A side of beef was placed upon the long demonstration table, and a Jefferson Market butcher separated it into the different "cuts" under Miss Parloa's direction. When the beef had been cut into the "hind" and "fore" quarters, Miss Parloa explained that it would be much easier to keep the different cuts in mind if a clear idea of the form and position of the bones of the animal were obtained. It was also a good plan to get the shape and direction of the backbone firmly fixed in the memory, and to take that as a starting point in learning the cuts.

"The muscles of the neck and legs and certain portions of the animal's body are used constantly," Miss Parloa continued, "and as they are continually contracting and expanding, they become much tougher than other portions of the body. But they are also richer and more juicy than those portions which are tenderer, because there is a freer flow of blood and nutriment to the muscles that are more often exercised. Keeping that in mind, and thinking of the animal as standing and moving, it is easy to remember what portions are tougher but more nutritious than others, and what portions are tenderer but less nutritious than others. This is the loin, as you see, and this the round, while from the loin extends this piece called the flank and inside flank. The inside flank is used largely for corning, braising or rolling and stuffing. For stuffing, roll it up after making a dressing for it of rolled crackers, salt and pepper, and take off all the suet, while leaving the fat, as the suet gives a disagreeable flavor to it. Tie the roll in a cloth, just cover it with boiling water and let it simmer slowly till done. Then let it get perfectly cold before cutting it in slices. Imbedded in this roll of suet here are the kidneys, which are nutritious and palatable if properly cooked. Beneath the kidneys and suet is the tenderloin. This is a layer of flesh which is used scarcely at all in muscular action and is kept very warm by these thick layers of suet, so that there is very little juice or nutrition in it. You have to lard it or use highly spiced sauces or dressings to make it palatable, and it is not fit to be given to sick persons. For corned beef the more fat you have on it the better, as the fat keeps the nutritious juices of the meat from being drawn out into the brine. So I think that it is really more economical to buy a very fat piece of beef for corn-

ing, although none of your family will eat fat corned beef, because you save so much of the nutrition and can try out the fat after it is corned for use as shortening and for other similar purposes. If you wish to make clear soup from the lower part of the leg, do not boil much bone or gristle with the meat, and do not boil it long, because the lime of the bone will soon begin to dissolve and will whiten the soup. I should think, however, that the whitened soup obtained from boiling the bones would be good for children on account of the lime which it would contain. The end of the loin toward the ribs you see grows gradually smaller. It is called the small porterhouse. The other end is called the large porterhouse. When the hindquarter and about seven ribs from the forequarter are cut off, you have about all the choice portions of the animal. There is very little demand for the other parts, because they are tough. If you are going to give a dinner-party and wish to have a fillet of tenderloin, I would advise you to buy a very large piece of the loin, which you can get for a reasonable price, between 25 and 30 cents a pound, according to time and place. Then use the layer of tenderloin for your fillet, and you will have all the rest to use for steaks or for a fine roast. For the fillet alone you would have to pay $1 a pound and would have nothing left. Of course that plan is economical only for a large family which can soon consume a large roast or a number of large steaks. If you are not going to give a large dinner-party where you wish to have specially handsome dishes, don't think about a fillet. Don't give it to your own family or especially to your children, for, as I have already said, it contains no nutriment. If you have a large family you will find it more economical to buy the flank or ribs that extend from the sirloin, or a rib-roast, together with the roast. For you get the whole piece at a much lower price than that which you must pay for the roast with the ends cut off, and you can use the best part for the meat, while the flank or ribs you can use for corning, boiling, potting, brazing, rolling or for soup stock. It is important to remember that steak will not be tender unless it is cut across the grain of the meat by the butcher. There is a layer on the top of the loin the fibre of which runs in a different direction from the rest of the loin. As steaks are commonly cut this is tough but juicy and nutritious. If it is cut off separately from the rest and across its grain it makes one of the finest, tenderest and at the same time the juiciest and most nutritious steak in the whole animal. There is another small portion which is just as good, however. It is a cube of meat on the top of the round, near where the loin begins. This is the best piece in the animal for making beef-tea for invalids. The round, as you see, is divided by the bone and a thin layer of fat into an upper and a lower portion. The lower portion is always tough, as its muscles are much used. The upper portion is tender and makes better steaks, while the lower part is better for potting and similar uses.

"The final cut from the fore quarter gives the rib roasts, which are economical for a small family. At the seventh rib, where the shoulder blade begins to appear, the meat is not so tender. These delicate pieces called the skirt are good for rolling and for beef-tea and should be cooked slowly for a long time. The best animals are those which have a large amount of meat—not fat, necessarily—in proportion to the amount of bones. The meat is of a finer grain and is more juicy and nutritious in such an animal than in one with large bones and comparatively little meat. Cross-rib meats, as they are called, are very nice, many think, for soup, stews, braising or pot-roasts. In mutton and veal the cutlets come from the ribs and from the legs. The skin of the cutlets from the leg should be notched all around to prevent the meat from bulging out when broiling, as it often does."

VII.

CROQUETTES, CHOPS, VEGETABLES, ROYAL DIPLOMATIC PUDDING, ETC.

A talk about croquettes occupied the first half hour of Miss Parloa's morning public object lesson. Directions for making chicken croquettes have already been given. Lobster croquettes are made in much the same way. When two tablespoonfuls of butter and half a tablespoonful of flour have been cooked together until they bubble, there should be added a scant half cupful of cream or water, the meat of a two pound lobster, chopped fine, and salt and pepper to suit the taste. When these ingredients become hot an egg, well beaten, should be added. The mixture should be cooled, and portions of it should be shaped like cylinders, dipped into beaten egg and cracker crumbs, and fried.

Sweet potato croquettes are an especially palatable sweet entrée, Miss Parloa said. To make them she mixed together two cupfuls of cold boiled and grated sweet potato, three tablespoonfuls of melted butter, a teaspoonful of lemon juice, one-fourth of a cupful of cream, one and a half teaspoonfuls of salt, one-fourth of a teaspoonful of pepper, one teaspoonful of sugar and a slight grating of nutmeg. The mixture was beaten until light and smooth. Portions of it were shaped in the same way as for lobster croquettes, rolled lightly in crumbs, then dipped into the beaten egg (two eggs were used), rolled once in crumbs, and fried a minute and a half in boiling fat. Miss Parloa suggested that the croquettes may be served, if one choose, with a pint of thin cream, seasoned lightly with salt, pepper and nutmeg and heated just to the boiling point.

Several French chops were seasoned with pepper and salt, dipped in melted butter and rolled in fine bread crumbs, and broiled over a bright fire—not extremely bright, because the crumbs are easily set afire. Potato balls—cut from cooked potatoes with a vegetable scoop and fried in washed butter or in chicken fat—may be served with these chops. On this occasion, however, Miss Parloa pared a dozen potatoes of medium size and, after allowing them to stand in water for some minutes to freshen them, boiled them for a quarter of an hour. She added a tablespoonful of salt and continued the boiling for fifteen minutes. Every drop of water was then poured off and the saucepan was shaken in a current of cold air. The potatoes were mashed until fine and light, and to them were added a tablespoonful of butter and half a tablespoonful of salt. After a good beating an addition was made of half a cupful of boiling milk. The potato was beaten like cake for a considerable time, and when served with the chops, or cutlets, it was delicate.

That homely vegetable, the carrot, can easily be prepared in a most toothsome way, as was soon shown. Two large carrots were scraped and cut into dice, balls, and long, slender strips, and these were cooked for an hour in a kettle containing two quarts of water. The water was then poured off, and the pieces of carrot were put into a saucepan together with half a cupful of white stock, one teaspoonful of salt, and a little pepper. After ten minutes' simmering, a tablespoonful of butter was added, and the dish was allowed to boil up once. Most of it was served at once; part was put aside for awhile.

For peas à la Française Miss Parloa used a pan of French peas. They were heated and drained. A tablespoonful of flour, twice as much butter and half a teaspoonful of sugar were stirred in a saucepan until thoroughly mixed. The peas were added, and the stirring over the fire was continued for five minutes, when a cupful of cream was added. The peas were simmered for ten minutes. Had they been fresh peas they would have boiled until tender instead of being simply heated through. Upon the dish were heaped little groups of the fancifully-shaped pieces of carrot that had been reserved.

In the afternoon the audience first gave attention to the making of a royal diplomatic pudding. Half a box of gelatine had been soaked an hour or more in half a cupful of cold water, and upon it was poured two-thirds of a pint of boiling water. Half a pint of wine, the juice of a lemon and a cupful of sugar were added, and the mixture was stirred and strained. Upon the table stood two moulds, one holding two quarts and the other half as much. A layer of jelly was put into the larger would, which was at once placed on ice. When the jelly became hard it was garnished with candied cherries cut in two. A few spoonfuls of the liquid jelly—which Miss Parloa was careful to ascertain was not hot—were poured into the mould to hold the cherries in position, and afterward enough more was poured in to cover them. When all the jelly had hardened, the smaller mould was set into the larger and the space between the sides of the two was filled with jelly. Ice was packed into the small mould, and the large mould was set in a basin of ice-water. When the last of the jelly had become solid the ice was removed from the small mould, and warm water took its place. This made it easy to lift the mould from the jelly a moment later. The space left vacant was filled with a custard made of these materials: Half a cupful of gelatine (previously soaked in half a cupful of cold water), half a cupful of sugar, the yolks of five eggs, two tablespoonfuls of wine, a scant cupful of milk, a teaspoonful of vanilla extract. The milk was boiled. To it were added the eggs and sugar, beaten together, and the gelatine. The mixture was strained, and the vanilla and wine were added. When the custard began to thicken, there was added half a pint of cream whipped to a stiff froth. The custard was poured into the vacant space mentioned and was allowed to stand until hard. The pudding was then turned out of the mould and served with soft custard poured around it. For this custard there were used the yolks of eight eggs and whites of two, a quart of milk, a scant half teaspoonful of sugar, half a teaspoonful of salt, and a teaspoonful of lemon extract. The eggs and sugar having been beaten together, a cupful of the milk was added. The remainder was heated to the boiling point and poured upon the beaten mixture, which was at once put upon the stove in a double boiler. The custard was stirred until it began to thicken—say about five minutes—and the salt was added. The custard was set away to cool, and when it was cold the flavor was added. The audience was cautioned against lifting carelessly the smaller of the two moulds used in making the pudding. Miss Parloa said it would be better to melt the jelly a trifle more in order to raise the mould easily than it would be to raise the mould quickly, and possibly jar the jelly so much as to mar the appearance of the dish. She said, also, that the space from which the smaller mould was taken must be filled slowly with the preparation designed for it.

Between the stages of work on the royal diplomatic pudding Miss Parloa made two other dishes. For *biscuit glacé*, half a cupful of water and two-thirds of a cupful of sugar were first boiled together for half an hour. Three eggs were beaten well and stirred into the boiling syrup, and the saucepan containing this mixture was placed in another of boiling water. For eight minutes the mixture was vigorously beaten; then the saucepan was transferred from the pan of hot water to one of cold water, and the mixture was beaten until cold. A teaspoonful of vanilla extract and a pint of cream whipped to a froth, were added and the mixture was again stirred well. It was put into little paper cases, shaped like cake pans and three or four inches long. These were made by Miss Parloa, who said they could be bought at the best restaurateurs if one did not choose to make them at home. A dozen and a half macaroons were browned in the oven, and after they had been cooled and had become hard on account of these processes, they were rolled fine. A layer of the crumbs was put on the cream in each case. All the cases were carefully placed in an ice-cream freezer and buried in ice and salt; being allowed to remain buried a long time.

For coffee jelly, a box of gelatine was soaked nearly two hours in half a pint of cold water. A pint and a half of boiling water was poured upon it, and when it had been wholly dissolved, a pint of

sugar and a pint of strong (cooked) coffee were added. The jelly was strained, poured into a border mould, and set away to harden. In due time, when it was turned out, sweetened and whipped cream was heaped within the circle of jelly.

In making the next dish, ham toast, Miss Parloa's first step was to cut cold boiled lean ham into thin slices and then into dice, and she said incidentally that if people would always cut meat or vegetables into slices, then put the slices together and cut them into strips, and finally cut across the strips at proper intervals, they would avoid giving the meat or vegetables that mashed appearance which is so common when they are cut up in the chopping-tray. The work can be done rapidly and all of the pieces are of about equal size. Resuming her work she seasoned a cupful of the ham with salt, pepper, a "speck" of cayenne and a quarter of a teaspoonful of dry mustard. She put a tablespoonful of butter into a small frying-pan, and when it was hot she added a teaspoonful of flour. After stirring until the mixture was smooth and frothy she added two-thirds of a cupful of stock; stirring all the while until it boiled up. This she seasoned with pepper, and salt. The ham was added, and cooked five minutes, with an occasional stirring. As soon as it was hot it was spread upon slices of toasted bread, and served.

The last dish prepared was ham and eggs on toast. Trimmings from cold boiled ham were cut fine and spread upon buttered slices of toast. These were put into the oven for about three minutes. In the meantime six eggs and half a cupful of milk were beaten together, and a teaspoonful of salt and a little pepper were added. Two tablespoonfuls of butter were put into the saucepan with the mixture, and when this had been heated so much that it thickened it was taken off, beaten for a moment and spread over the ham and toast.

VIII.

SWEETBREADS, PUDDINGS, FOOD FOR THE SICK.

"We will first make a Danish pudding," said Miss Parloa, addressing her audience. "This cupful of tapioca was washed yesterday and has been soaking through the night in three pints of water, measured liberally. I will put it in the double-boiler and cook it for an hour, stirring it often. I shall then add half a teacupful of sugar, half a teaspoonful of salt and this tumbler of bright jelly, mixing all together thoroughly. The pudding will be put into a mould that has been dipped in cold water, and be set away to harden; and by and by you shall eat it with sugar and cream."

While the Danish pudding was cooking a Swiss pudding was begun. The rind of a lemon was grated into a pint of milk, which was put upon the stove in a double boiler. A teacupful of flour and four tablespoonfuls of butter having been rubbed together, the milk was poured upon them as soon as it boiled. All the ingredients were put into the boiler to be cooked five minutes, with a stirring during the first two. The yolks of five eggs and three tablespoonfuls of sugar were beaten together and stirred into the boiling mixture, which was immediately thereafter removed from the fire and set away to cool. When it had become cold the whites of the eggs, beaten to a stiff froth, were added. The pudding was turned into a three-quart mould that had been carefully buttered, and steamed for forty minutes, when it was turned out upon a hot dish and served at once.

Creamy sauce accompanied this pu'ding. Half a cupful of butter was beaten to a cream, and, while the beating was continued, half a cupful of powdered sugar was gradually added. When the mixture was light and creamy four tablespoonfuls of wine were added, and then one-fourth of a cupful of cream, a little at a time. When the sauce had been beaten smooth the bowl containing it was set into a basin of hot water, and the stirring was resumed until the sauce was perfectly smooth and creamy—no longer. This condition was secured in a few moments.

Early in the course of the lesson Miss Parloa had put a cupful of rice on to boil in three cupfuls of water, and she now said that as it had boiled half an hour she would, as a second step in the making of a rice border, add a heaping teaspoonful of salt and two tablespoonfuls of butter, and set the rice back where it would simmer for an hour. She next spoke of sweetbreads, which are found in calves and lambs, near the throat or the heart. All the tough skin should be carefully pulled off, she said, and the sweetbreads should be allowed to lie in cold water for ten minutes. They should afterward be boiled for twenty minutes, no matter what the subsequent mode of cooking is to be.

Miss Parloa first showed how to lard and bake them. Through each she drew four pieces of pork about the size of a match. She let the sweetbreads lie in cold water for five or more minutes and boiled them twenty minutes, after which she spread them with butter, dredged them with pepper, salt and flour, and baked them twenty minutes in a quick oven. The way to broil was next shown. Sweetbreads were split, and were seasoned with pepper and salt, rubbed with butter and sprinkled with flour. They were broiled over a quick fire for ten minutes, being constantly turned. For a *sauté*, a single sweetbread was split and cut into four pieces, which were seasoned with salt and pepper. A small tablespoonful of butter and a like quantity of flour having been heated in a frying-pan, the sweetbread was put in, and was turned constantly until lightly browned. About eight minutes were required to cook it.

Cream sauce was served with the sweetbreads in each instance. A pint of cream, less half a cupful, was heated to the boiling point, and into it was stirred a generous tablespoonful of flour mixed smooth with the half-cupful of cream that was reserved from the pint. Pepper and salt were added, and the same was boiled for three minutes.

Miss Parloa again gave her attention to the rice border. The rice was mashed very fine with a spoon and, after two well-beaten eggs had been added, was stirred for three minutes. A plain border mould having been heated, the rice was turned into it and heated for ten minutes. It was then put where it would keep warm, and chocolate pies were made. Half a cupful of butter was beaten until light, and to it was gradually added a cupful of sugar. The butter was beaten all the while, and a cream was soon formed. Three eggs were beaten till light, and were added, together with a cupful of milk, to the creamy mixture. All the materials then received a thorough mixing. Three cupfuls of flour, with which a teaspoonful of soda and two of cream of tartar had been mixed, were stirred into the first mixture, which was then flavored with lemon. Washington-pie plates were filled, and the cakes were baked about twenty minutes. When done they were split, and upon one-half was spread a filling made from this recipe: Mix together a square of Baker's chocolate, scraped, and a cupful of sugar, and add, very slowly, one-third of a cupful of boiling milk and the yolks of two eggs; simmer for ten minutes, taking care that the mixture does not burn; flavor with vanilla and have it perfectly cold before using. The two parts of the pie were put together, and powdered sugar was sprinkled upon the upper part.

The last dish made was a blanquette of veal. A quart of cooked veal, cut into small pieces, was used; also, a cupful of cream, a large cupful of white stock, the yolks of four eggs, three tablespoonfuls of butter, a heaping tablespoonful of flour, a teaspoonful of lemon-juice, and small quantities of salt and pepper. The butter was put into a sauce-pan, and when it was hot the flour was added. The mixture was stirred until smooth but not brown. The stock was added; followed two minutes later by the cream and seasoning. As soon as the mixture had boiled up, the veal was put in, to be cooked ten minutes, at the end of which time the yolks of the eggs, beaten together with four tablespoonfuls of milk, were stirred into the blanquette, and the dish was cooked a moment longer. It was served in the rice-border previously prepared.

"Food for the sick" was the topic of the afternoon talk, and Scotch broth was the first dish made. Miss Parloa said this was excellent for convalescents, being appetizing and nutritious. Among the ingredients was a two-pound piece of the scraggy part of a neck of mutton. This particular cut was employed because the muscles of a sheep's neck are in such constant use as to make that part of the animal better-flavored and more nutritious than those parts through which the blood has run less freely. Miss Parloa cut the meat from the bones and removed all the fat. She cut the meat into small pieces and put it into a soup kettle, together with two slices of carrot, a slice of turnip, a stalk of celery and an onion—all cut fine, half a cupful of barley and three pints of water; and the broth was allowed to simmer gently for two hours. The bones, with a pint of water added, also were allowed the same amount of time for simmering, and the liquor was strained into the soup kettle. A tablespoonful each of butter and flour were cooked together until perfectly smooth, and then stirred into the broth; after which salt and pepper and a teaspoonful of chopped parsley were added.

The audience was cautioned against rapid cooking as a high temperature hardens the fibres of the meat, whereas a slow bubbling renders the meat tender and secures a better flavor for the broth. The vegetables should be cut very fine. Mutton is so nutritious and so easily digested as to deserve much attention as a food during convalescence. If it be properly cooked the peculiar flavor that is disagreeable to some people is concealed, though the meat remains palatable.

Mutton broth, which was recommended for patients whose food must be light, was next made. A pound of meat like that used for the Scotch broth was freed of fat and cut into small pieces and was put into a saucepan containing a quart of cold water. When this water had become heated to the boiling point it was carefully skimmed. A tablespoonful of barley was added, and the broth was simmered slowly for two hours.

In anticipation of making lemon jelly, Miss Parloa had soaked one-fourth of a cupful of gelatine in one-fourth of a cupful of cold water for two hours. She now poured upon the gelatine a cupful of boiling water and added half a cupful of sugar and one-fourth of a cupful of lemon juice, and after straining the jelly through a napkin into a mould, she set it away to harden.

For an oyster stew, the liquor was drained from half a pint of oysters and allowed to heat to the boiling point, when it was skimmed. In the meantime, half a pint of milk was heated to the boiling point in the double-boiler. Into it were stirred a teaspoonful of butter, the proper quantity of salt to give the stew a good flavor, and the oysters. The dish was boiled up once, and served immediately.

Miss Parloa cautioned her hearers against overcooking oysters at any time. She then selected a number of large ones, drained them, seasoned them with salt and pepper, dipped them in melted butter and dredged them with flour. She broiled them over a quick fire until the edges curled, and served them on buttered toast.

After some English snipe had been cleaned the wings were cut off, as well as the legs at the first joint. The birds were cut open in the back, seasoned with salt and pepper, dipped in melted butter and dredged with flour. They were broiled eight or ten minutes, and served on buttered toast.

Cream toast was next made. Half a cupful of cream was heated to the boiling point and seasoned with salt. In the meantime two slices of bread were nicely browned. They were dipped in the cream and placed on a dish, and the remaining cream was poured over them.

For cracker gruel, a scant half pint of boiling water was poured upon four tablespoonfuls of powdered cracker, and, after half a pint of milk and half a teaspoonful of salt had been added, the mixture was stirred until it had boiled up once.

Last of all, eggnog was made. The white of an egg was beaten to a stiff froth; next a tablespoonful of sugar was beaten in; then the yolk of the egg, and finally a tablespoonful each of milk, water and wine.

Before closing, Miss Parloa said that when using milk in dishes for the sick the diseases of the persons who are to consume the food should be considered. Long boiling hardens the albumen and makes the milk constipating, hence, if the patient be already constipated, great care should be exercised not to allow the milk or cream to heat above the boiling point. Miss Parloa said also that one could not use seasonings for a sick person that would suit a well person. More salt and acid can and should be used in most cases when seasoning food for the sick, while less sugar or other sweet flavor should be used. Advice was also given not to send a too bountiful supply of food to the patient, and not to set any one dish before him frequently just because it has tasted especially good at first. Miss Parloa emphasized the desirability of serving all dishes in the daintiest and most attractive ways, so as to induce an appetite which may be dormant.

IX.

BREAKFAST DISHES, BAVARIAN CREAM, WINE JELLY, ETC.

" These are my last public lessons in New-York this season," said Miss Parloa. "I shall devote my time for the present to my courses of lectures out of town, but shall resume the giving of demonstration lessons and private instructions here in the fall." She announced that the morning's topic was " Breakfast Dishes," and that salt fish soufflé would be prepared first. Eight good-sized potatoes had previously been pared and then boiled for half an hour. The water was carefully poured off, and the potatoes were mashed fine and mixed with a pint of fine-chopped cooked salt fish. Three-fourths of a cupful of hot milk, two generous tablespoonfuls of butter, and small quantities of salt and pepper were added. Two eggs were heaten and stirred in, and the mixture was heaped upon the dish on which it was to be served, and placed in the oven for ten minutes. The whites of two more eggs were beaten to a stiff froth. A quarter of a teaspoonful of salt was added and then the yolks. This preparation was spread upon the dish of fish, which was browned in the oven, and served at once.

A cupful of hominy was washed in two waters and stirred into a quart of boiling water. A teaspoonful of salt was added, and the dish was boiled for nearly an hour. Miss Parloa mixed together a pint of the warm hominy, a pint of milk and a pint of flour, and after beating two eggs, she stirred them into the batter, adding a little salt at the time. Of this batter excellent griddle cakes were made; the griddle being very hot to prevent the cakes from being tough.

For hominy muffins, a teacupful of boiling water was poured upon two tablespoonfuls of fine uncooked hominy. After fifteen minutes' simmering this mixture was added to one consisting of a cupful and a half of boiling milk and a cupful of Indian meal. The combined mixtures were allowed to cool, and when they were cool there were added to them two well-beaten eggs, two tablespoonfuls of sugar and a teaspoonful each of salt and baking-powder. The batter was poured into small pans that had been heated and buttered. Fifteen minutes' baking gave delicious muffins.

The first step in the making of corn muffins was to mix together in a sieve, and finally rub through it, a teacupful of cornmeal, twice as much flour, a third of a cupful of sugar, a teaspoonful of salt, and three teaspoonfuls of baking-powder. Having put two tablespoonfuls of butter into a cup, Miss Parloa set the cup into a basin of hot water; and while the butter was melting, she beat three eggs very light and added to them a large cupful of milk. This mixture she poured upon the dry ingredients, beating well all the while. The melted butter was added, and the mixture was poured into buttered muffin pans and baked twenty minutes. Miss Parloa used white meal for these muffins, but said that yellow would have given about as good a result.

Several fine slices of halibut, about an inch, thick, having been seasoned with salt and pepper and allowed to lie in melted butter—covering both sides—for half an hour, were rolled in flour, and broiled for twelve minutes over a clear fire. The halibut was served on a hot dish with a handsome garnish of parsley and slices of lemon. Miss Parloa said that about three tablespoonfuls of melted butter should be allowed for each pound of the uncooked fish.

Halibut was also served with maître d'hôtel butter, which was made by beating four tablespoonfuls of butter to a cream and gradually beating into it a tablespoonful each of lemon juice and vinegar a teaspoonful of chopped parsley, half a teaspoonful of salt and a quarter of a teaspoonful of pepper. Both sides of a broiler having been buttered, the slices of halibut, seasoned with salt and pepper, were cooked over clear coals for twelve minutes, receiving a turning frequently. The fish was placed upon a hot dish, and over it was spread the maître d'hôtel butter; a spoonful being used for each pound of fish.

Liver was cooked in a variety of ways. First, slices were dipped in butter and lightly in flour, and broiled eight or ten minutes over a bright fire.

A pound of liver was cut into small thin pieces, and after four tablespoonfuls of butter had been heated, the meat was cooked in it slowly for four

minutes. Two tablespoonfuls of flour, a teaspoonful of curry powder, two slices of onion, a "speck" of cayenne and small quantities of salt and pepper were added, and after two minutes' cooking a cupful of stock was slowly added. The dish, after it had once boiled up, was announced to be a curry of liver.

For liver sauté, liver was cut into very thin slices, and seasoned with salt and pepper. Two tablespoonfuls of butter and a large tablespoonful of flour were heated together in a small frying-pan, and the liver was laid in and browned on both sides. Two tablespoonfuls of water, one of wine, and a tablespoonful of chopped parsley were added, and after Miss Parloa had tasted of the dish, to ascertain if it were salt enough, she boiled it up once, and served it.

A pint of potato balls were cut out of raw potatoes with a vegetable scoop, and boiled gently for twelve minutes. The water was drained from them, and a cupful of boiling milk substituted. A teaspoonful of butter, a like quantity of chopped parsley and a scant teaspoonful of salt were added, and the dish was allowed to simmer eight minutes.

"We will begin with wine jelly," said Miss Parloa at her next lecture. A box of gelatine had been soaked two hours in half a pint of cold water. Upon it was poured a pint and a half of boiling water, and a stirring followed until the gelatine was dissolved. A pint of sugar, a pint of sherry and the juice of a lemon were added, and part of the jelly was strained through a napkin into a border mould. When it had become slightly hardened—a bed of ice being used to promote the hardening—a row of fresh strawberries was laid upon it. A little more jelly was poured in, to hold the fruit in place; and when it had become somewhat solid the remainder of the jelly was added, and the mould put into the ice chest.

The making of a bird's-nest pudding next absorbed the attention of the audience. The jelly for it had been prepared at the same time as the wine jelly, the processes being similar. Half a package of sparkling gelatine had been soaked for two hours in half a cupful of cold water, and upon it had been poured enough boiling water to make, with the juice of six oranges, two cupfuls and a half of liquor. After this water and orange juice and a small cupful of sugar had been added, the jelly had been stirred well, and strained into a shallow dish. This was where it was found when Miss Parloa announced that a bird's-nest pudding was in order. A plate of "straws" was produced, and it was explained that they were obtained in this way: Peel was removed from half a dozen oranges in quarters, and allowed to lie over night in two quarts of water. The next morning the peel was cut into thin strips with scissors, and boiled in fresh water until tender. The strips were drained in a sieve, and simmered half an hour in a syrup made of half a cupful of sugar and a pint of water. They were then put into a bowl, and remained there over night. On the day of the lecture a pint of sugar and of water were boiled together for twenty minutes, and the syrup fell in threads from a spoon with which a quantity was dipped up.

The orange peel straws were boiled half an hour in this syrup, and then removed and drained in a sieve. As they became dry they were put into a dish and placed in a warm oven.

Thus a large part of the work was done before the lecture, but each finished step was explained with much care. Miss Parloa put into a double-boiler a pint of milk and a third of a box of gelatine that had been soaking for two hours, and heated the mixture without allowing it to boil. She gave it a stirring frequently As soon as the gelatine had been dissolved the mixture was removed from the fire, and to it were added one and a half table-spoonfuls of sugar, a third of a teaspoonful of orange flavor, and a tiny quantity of salt. This blanc-mange was poured into six egg shells that had been emptied by breaking in one end a hole about the size of a cent, and stirring a skewer inside. The shells were placed upright in a pan of fine-powdered ice. The jelly that had been prepared was broken into pieces with a fork and put into a flat dish. The straws were arranged in the form of nests on the jelly, the shells were taken from the blanc-mange, and the eggs of blanc-mange were placed in the nests.

Miss Parloa said at this point that when gelatine is to be used it should be soaked in cold water, standing in a cold place, for two hours, for it will then dissolve readily without being brought to a high temperature, which is likely to give a strong flavor. The vessel in which the gelatine is dissolved should not be put directly upon the range, but into another containing hot water, and this may be put upon the range.

For strawberry Bavarian cream there were used a pint of cream, a quart of strawberries, half a cupful of cold water, half a cupful of boiling water, a large cupful of sugar and half a package of gelatine. The gelatine had soaked two hours in the cold water, and the berries and sugar had been mashed together and allowed to stand for an hour. The cream was now whipped to a froth. The juice from the berries was strained as much as possible, being pressed through; but care was taken that none of the seeds went with it. The hot water was poured upon the gelatine, which, when it was dissolved, was strained into the strawberry juice. The basin (which was tin) was set into a pan of ice water, and the mixture was beaten until a cream had formed. When it was of about the consistence of soft custard, the whipped cream was stirred into it; and after a good stirring the mixture was turned into moulds and set away to harden.

Corn-starch cake was made by beating a cupful of butter to a cream and adding a cupful and a half of flour, four eggs well beaten, half a cupful of corn-starch dissolved in half a cupful of milk, and a cup and a half of flour into which had been stirred a teaspoonful of cream-of-tartar and half a teaspoon-

ful of soda; the mixture being flavored with lemon and baked in two sheets.

After making this cake Miss Parloa turned the mould of wine jelly into a glass dish, and turned the Bavarian cream into the circle of jelly, heaping whipped cream about it.

This ended the last public lesson. Miss Parloa was congratulated on having excited a considerable amount of interest in cookery during the brief season her school had been open. Some of the ladies present had attended nearly every lesson, and expressed not only the feeling that they had been more than repaid for devoting so much time and thought to the culinary art, but the intention of being regular auditors when the school should be opened in the fall.

HOUSEHOLD NOTES.

POT AU FEU.—Take a good-sized beef-bone with plenty of meat on it, extract the marrow and place in a pot on the back of the range, covering the beef with three or more quarts of cold water; cover tightly and allow to simmer all day long. The next day, before heating, remove the grease from the top, and add a large onion which has been stuck full of cloves and roasted in the oven till of a rich brown color; then add any other vegetables which one may fancy. Rice or vermicelli may be added for a change. Just before serving, burn a little brown sugar and stir through it. This gives a peculiar flavor and rich color to the soup.

BUNS.—Two quarts of warm water, two pounds of sugar, one and a half pounds of butter, two ounces of allspice, six eggs beaten by themselves, one pint of yeast. Put the flour, yeast and water together about as thick as pudding, set it by the fire, let it rise to a sponge, and mix the sugar and butter together. Then beat the whole together after rising and knead in flour enough but not very stiff; make the buns small and brush them over with egg just as you put them into the oven.

CUP CAKE.—Five cups of flour, three of sugar, one of butter, one of cream, five eggs, one teaspoonful of soda; season to taste.

RICE WAFFLES.—One quart of flour; half a teaspoonful of salt; one teaspoonful of sugar; two teaspoonfuls of baking-powder; one large table-spoonful of butter; two eggs; one and a half pints of milk; one cupful of hot boiled rice. Sift the flour, salt, sugar and baking-powder well together; rub the butter into the flour, beat the eggs well, separately, and add the stiff whites last of all.

WHITEBAIT.—Drain them on a clean napkin until the water is thoroughly absorbed. Roll them in flour and drop them into a deep pan of hot lard; let them remain in it until crisp, then with a slice remove them from the fat, and put them on a sieve to drain. Dry them for a few minutes before the fire, sprinkle a little salt over them and serve them on a napkin. Slices of very thin brown bread and butter, and lemons cut in quarters, and Cayenne pepper are handed around with them.

PINEAPPLE PUDDING.—Butter a pudding dish, and line the bottom and sides with slices of stale cake (sponge cake is best), pare and slice thin a large pineapple; place in the dish first a layer of pineapple, then strew with sugar, then more pineapple, and so on until is used. Pour over a small teacupful of water, and cover with slices of cake which have been dipped in cold water; cover the whole with a buttered plate, and bake slowly for two hours.

KISSES.—Whites of six eggs; one pound of pulverized sugar, one drop of rose oil. Put the sugar in the dish first, and drop the whites of eggs (unbeaten upon it. Beat them together thoroughly for two hours. Drop on tins with a teaspoon, turning spoon round and round until the cakes are very high and end in a point; this will give them a fluted appearance. When baked and still hot, stick two of them together, using a little white of egg if necessary. Lay them very carefully upon an inverted sieve to cool. They may also be squeezed through a meringue bag like lady-fingers, or they may be dropped in smooth round cakes.

LEMON PUDDING.—Grate the peel of two lemons and add the juice of one; mix with two crackers. Add three-quarters of a pound of sugar, yolks of twelve eggs, whites of six, three-quarters of a pound of melted butter, half a pint of thick cream. Mix well together, line the dish with a very thick paste, pour the ingredients in and bake one hour.

EVE'S PUDDING.—Grate three-quarters of a pound of bread, three-quarters of a pound of suet, three-quarters of a pound of apples; three-quarters of a pound of currants, four eggs and the peel of a lemon grated, Put into shape and boil three hours. Serve with rich sauce.

ELECTION CAKE.—Five pounds flour, one and three-quarter pounds butter, two pounds sugar, two pounds stoned raisins, one nutmeg, half pint brandy, one gill sherry or Madeira wine, one pint yeast, one quart new milk. Rub part of the butter into the flour, as it would not rise so well with the whole, or melt it in the milk, as it rises better to be warm. Add the milk and yeast at night. If well risen in the morning, add the other ingredients: if not, let it stand till well risen. Flour, butter, milk and yeast to be put together at night.

BRAISED TONGUE.—Wash a fresh beef tongue, and, with a trussing needle, run a strong twine through the roots and end of it, drawing tightly enough to have the end meet the roots; then tie firmly. Cover with boiling water, and boil gently for two hours; then take up and drain. Put six tablespoonfuls of butter in the braising pan, and when hot put in half a small carrot, half a small turnip, and two onions, all cut fine. Cook five minutes stirring all the time, and then draw to one side. Roll the tongue in flour, and put in the pan. As soon as browned on one side, turn, and brown the other. Add one quart of the water in which it was boiled, a bouquet of sweet herbs, one clove, a small

piece of cinnamon, and salt and pepper. Cover, and cook two hours in a slow oven, basting often with the gravy in the pan, and salt, pepper, and flour. When it has been cooking an hour and a half, add the juice of half a lemon to the gravy. When done, take up. Melt two tablespoonfuls of glaze, and pour over the tongue. Place in the heater until the gravy is made. Mix one tablespoonful of cornstarch with a little cold water, and stir into the boiling gravy, of which there should be one pint. Boil one minute; then strain, and pour around the tongue. Garnish with parsley, and serve.

SNOW PUDDING.—Dissolve half a box of gelatine over night in one and a half pints of warm water. The next morning add the whites of four eggs, two scant teacupfuls of powdered sugar and one teaspoonful of extract of vanilla. Beat the mixture for an hour, then turn it into a mould and set it upon ice. Serve with golden sauce.

GOLDEN SAUCE.—Make a smooth boiled custard with the yolks of three eggs, half a cupful of sugar and a pint of milk. Flavor it to taste.

CREAM A LA VERSAILLES.—One quart of milk, half a cupful sugar, half a teaspoonful of vanilla extract, half a teaspoonful of salt, seven cups, two tablespoonfuls of water. Put the sugar in a small frying-pan and stir until a very light brown. Add the water, stir a moment longer, and mix with the milk. Beat the eggs and salt with a spoon. Add this mixture and the vanilla to the milk. Butter a two-quart charlotte russe mould lightly, and put the custard in it. Put the mould into a basin of warm (not hot) water and bake slowly until the custard is firm in the centre. It should take forty minutes; but if the oven is quite hot it will be done in thirty minutes. Test by putting a knife down into the centre, for if the custard is not milky, it is done. Set away in a cold place until serving time. It must be ice-cold when eaten. Turn out on a flat dish and pour caramel seed over it.

LOAF CAKE.—Two quarts of sugar, seven cupfuls of butter, six quarts of sifted flour, six pounds of fruit, one pint of wine, one pint of yeast, eight nutmegs, mace, twelve eggs, one quart of milk. It should be made at such an hour (being governed by the weather) as will give it time to get perfectly light by evening. It should stand about six hours in summer and eight in winter. Put in half the butter and eggs, and the milk, flavor and yeast, and beat thoroughly. In the evening add the remainder of the butter, rubbing it with the sugar, the rest of the eggs, and the spice. Let the cake rise again until morning; then add the fruit. Put in deep pans, and let rise about half an hour. Bake from two to three hours in a slow oven.

COOKIES.—Take one heaping cup of sugar, twelve tablespoonfuls of melted butter, six tablespoonfuls of hot water and one teaspoonful of soda. Mix quickly, with flour enough to roll; roll thin, and bake in quick oven on well-greased tins; keep in a stone jar.

CREAM CANDY.—One coffee-cupful of white sugar,

four tablespoonfuls of hot water to dissolve it; boil, without stirring, in a bright tin pan until it will crisp in water, like molasses candy. Just before it is done put in one-quarter teaspoonful of pure cream of tartar and a teaspoonful of essence of lemon, vanilla, or peppermint. When done, pour into a buttered pan, and when cool enough to handle, work like molasses candy until perfectly white; pull in strips of the thickness of your finger and cut in short pieces with the shears. Lay on buttered paper on plates.

POTATO CROQUETTES.—Season cold mashed potato with pepper, salt and nutmeg. Beat to a cream, with a tablespoonful of melted butter to every cupful of potato. Bind with two or three beaten eggs, and add some minced parsley. Roll into oval balls, dip in beaten egg, then in bread crumbs, and fry in hot lard er drippings. Pile in a pyramid upon a flat dish, and serve. They are nice with a little cream beaten up with them.

PRESSED VEAL.—Boil a beef tongue the day before it is used, and a like quantity of lean veal. Chop very fine. Season the tongue with pepper, powdered sweet herbs, a teaspoonful of mustard, a little nutmeg and cloves, a pinch of each; season the veal in like manner, with the addition of salt. Pack in alternate spoonfuls as irregularly as possible, in cups, bowls or jars which have been well buttered. Press very hard as you go on, smooth the top, and cover with melted butter. When this cools close the cans, and keep in a cool, dry place. Turn out whole, or cut in slices for tea. It is a pretty and savory relish, garnished with parsley or the blanched tops of celery.

BREADED EGGS.—Boil the eggs hard, and cut in round, thick slices; pepper and salt; dip each in beaten raw egg, then in fine bread crumbs or powdered cracker, and fry in nice dripping or butter, hissing hot. Drain off every drop of grease, and serve on a hot dish for breakfast, with sauce, like that for fricasseed eggs, poured over them.

NEAPOLITAN PUDDING—One large cup of fine bread crumbs soaked in milk; three-quarters of a cup of sugar; one lemon, juice and grated rind; six eggs; half a pound of stale sponge cake; half a pound of almond macaroons; half a cup of jelly or jam, and one small tumbler of sherry wine; one half cup of milk poured upon the bread crumbs; one teaspoonful of melted butter. Rub the butter and sugar together; put the beaten yolks in next; then the soaked bread crumbs, the lemon juice and rind, and beat to a smooth, light paste before adding the whites. Butter your mould very well, and put in the bottom a light layer of dry bread crumbs; upon this a layer of macaroons, laid evenly and closely together. Wet this with wine and cover with a layer of the mixture; then with slices of sponge cake, spread thickly with jelly or jam; next macaroons, wet with wine, more custard, sponge cake and jam, and so on until the mould is full, putting a layer of the mixture at the top. Cover closely, and steam in the oven three-quarters of an

hour; then remove the cover to brown the top. Turn out carefully into a dish, and pour over it a sauce made of currant jelly warmed and beaten up with two tablespoonfuls of melted butter and a glass of pale sherry.

FRITTERS.—One pint of flour, four eggs, one teaspoonful of salt, one pint of boiling water. Stir the flour into the water by degrees, and stir until it has boiled three minutes. Let it get almost cold, when beat in the yolks, then the whites of the eggs, which must be previously whipped stiff.

PRESERVED PINEAPPLE.—Pare, cut into slices, take out the core of each one, and weigh, allowing pound for pound of sugar and fruit. Put in alternate layers in the kettle and pour in water, allowing a teacupful to each pound of sugar. Heat to a boil; take out the pineapple and spread upon dishes in the sun. Boil and skim the syrup half an hour. Return the pineapple to the kettle and boil fifteen minutes. Take it out, pack in wide-mouthed jars, pour on the scalding syrup, cover to keep in the heat, and, when cold tie up, first putting brandied tissue-paper upon the top.

FIG LAYER CAKE.—Two cups of white sugar; one-half cup of butter; two and a half cups of flour; one cup of milk; two teaspoonfuls of baking-powder, and the whites of eight eggs; flavor with vanilla. For the filling take one cup of stoned raisins and one lemon, peeled; chop together; then add one-half-cup of water and one cup of sugar.

APPLE CUSTARD.—Peel and core eight or ten medium-sized apples; lay them in cold water until the syrup is prepared in which to boil them; make a syrup with a teacupful of water, the grated yellow rind and juice of one lemon, and a few pieces of stick cinnamon. When the syrup becomes clear put in the apples and simmer until soft. Take up the apples in in a draining spoon, and put them on the dish in which they are to be served; boil up the syrup and pour over them; make a soft custard with the yolks of four eggs, three tablespoonfuls of powdered sugar, and a scant quart of milk. When cold spread it over the apples. Whip the whites of the eggs, flavor with lemon, and place on the custard. Color in the oven.

STUFFED CABBAGE.—Take a large fresh cabbage and cut out the heart; fill the vacancy with stuffing made of cooked chicken or veal chopped very fine and highly seasoned, and rolled into balls with yolk of eggs. Tie the cabbage firmly together and boil in a covered kettle for two hours.

LOBSTER FRITTERS.—Cut the meat of a cold boiled lobster into dice and mix the lobster fat with it. Add three-quarters of a cupful of mushrooms cut into dice. Season this mixture with celery salt and cayenne pepper. Put a piece of butter, half the size of an egg, into a saucepan, and when it bubbles stir in a tablespoonful of flour. Let the flour cook a little, then add a cupful of cream and some finely minced parsley. Stir until the sauce thickens, then add the other ingredients, and stir well until they become scalding hot. Remove from the fire and stir in the well-beaten yolks of three eggs. Spread this mixture an inch thick upon a buttered dish and set it upon ice to become chilled. Then cut it into small parallelograms, and roll them in fritter batter, or beaten eggs and bread crumbs. Fry them in boiling lard.

VOLS-AU-VENT WITH STRAWBERRIES.—When the paté-shells are nearly baked draw them to the edge of the oven and brush the top over with white of egg beaten up with a little water and slightly sweetened. Sprinkle sugar over them, and return them to the oven. When they are done, fill them with fresh or preserved fruit, sprinkling a little sugar over fresh fruit. Serve them without the lids with a spoonful of whipped cream upon each patty.

PRUNE PUDDING.—Scald one pound of French prunes, let them swell in the hot water till soft, drain and extract the stones, spread on a dish and dredge with flour; take a gill of milk from a quart, stir into it gradually eight tablespoonfuls of sifted flour; beat six eggs very light and stir by degrees into remainder of the quart of milk, alternating with the batter; add prunes, one at a time; boil two hours and serve with wine sauce or cream.

COTTAGE PUDDING.—One cup of sugar; half cup butter; one egg; cup sweet milk; tablespoonful soda, dissolved in milk; two teaspoonful cream tartar in the flour; three cups flour; half teaspoonful extract of lemon. Sprinkle a little sugar over the top just before putting in the oven, bake in a small bread-pan, and when done cut in squares, and serve with sauce made of two tablespoonful butter, cup of sugar, tablespoonful flour wet with a little cold water and stirred until like cream; add a pint of boiling water, let boil two or three minutes, stirring all the time. After taking from the fire add half teaspoonful extract of lemon.

CLAM SOUP.—Fifty clams; one quart of milk; one pint of water; two tablespoonfuls of butter. Drain off the liquor from the clams and put it over the fire with a few bits of Cayenne pods, half a dozen blades of mace and salt to taste. Let it boil for ten minutes, then put in the clams and boil half an hour, keeping the pot closely covered. If you dislike to see the whole spices in the tureen, strain them out before the clams are added. At the end of the half hour add the milk, which has been heated to scalding, not boiling, in another vessel. Boil up again, taking care the soup does not burn, and put in the butter. Serve without delay.

LEMON CUSTARD.—Twelve eggs; twelve cupfuls of sugar; six lemons; one tablespoonful of flour; two teaspoonfuls of cream. Grate and squeeze the lemons, mix the sugar well with them, add the well-beaten yolks, then the flour, the cream, and last of all, the well-beaten whites. Bake in pie-plates, lined with rich puff paste.

CALF'S BRAINS A LA MILANAISE.—Wash the brains carefully and boil them until tender in salted boiling water. Mash them into a smooth paste and season well with pepper, salt, grated onion, and a little chopped parsley. Moisten the mixture slightly with melted butter, then stiffen it a little with cracker or bread crumbs. Add one or two well-beaten eggs to bind it, then set it upon ice to become quite cold. Form the mixture into small round cakes and fry them delicately in hot butter. Arrange them in the centre of a hot platter and place around them a border of *spaghetti* (maccaroni) cooked and dressed with tomato sauce, flavored with onion.

ROYAL CROQUETTES.—Roast a plump, tender chicken, and when cool, chop the white meat as fine as possible, then pound to a smooth paste. Scald a sweetbread and remove the sinews. Fry it brown in butter, then let it cool. Pound it to a smooth paste and add it to the chicken. Season to taste with pepper and salt, and add a well-beaten egg. Moisten it with rich cream, and work into it a teaspoonful of flour to give it consistency. Stir it well over the fire until it becomes hot, then spread it upon a buttered dish to cool. Form the mixture into cork-shaped croquettes, and egg, bread crumb, and fry them in the usual way.

NEAPOLITAN CAKE.—Dark part: One cupful of butter; two cupfuls of brown sugar; one cupful of molasses; one cupful of strong, cold coffee; four and a half cupfuls of flour; four eggs; two teaspoonfuls of soda well sifted with the flour; two teaspoonfuls of powdered cloves; two teaspoonfuls of cinnamon; one teaspoonful of powdered mace; one pound of stoned raisins; half a pound of chopped figs; half a pound of well washed and dried currants. Bake in jelly-cake pans.

White part: One cupful of butter; four cupfuls of flour; four cupfuls of sugar; two cupfuls of sweet milk; two cupfuls of corn-starch; whites of eight eggs; six teaspoonfuls of baking powder; flavor to taste with bitter almond. Bake in jelly-cake pans. Grate the peel and squeeze the juice from two lemons; add enough pulverized sugar to stiffen the juice; spread it between the cakes, using alternately a white and a dark cake. Frost the top and sides of the cake with lemon icing.

FRESH PINEAPPLE.—When properly prepared this is a delicious fruit for dessert, but as usually served eat round in slices it is naught. It should be carefully peeled and all the "eyes" taken out in the morning of the day on which it is to be used. Leave the topmost plume of green leaves, and set the fruit on the dish in which it is to be served. Then dust it thickly with powdered sugar and let it stand until it is to be served. Tear it apart with a fork, holding the plume of green leaves with the left hand. This mode of serving insures the retention of the rich juices.

LAMB CUTLETS A LA CONDE.—Cut and trim a dish of cutlets from a neck of lamb. Lard them thickly with small strips of truffles, anchovies and gherkins, and surround each cutlet with a seasoning made with fine bread crumbs, mushrooms, a few chives, a small quantity of shalots, some capers, the yolks and whites of two hard-boiled eggs, all chopped very fine, and moistened with olive oil and a small piece of butter, till of a proper consistency,

Add pepper and salt to taste. Keep the seasoning in place on each cutlet with a small piece of the transparent skin that covers the fat in the inside of the lamb, and fix the cutlets to a small spit, covering them with oiled or buttered paper. Cook them in front of a clear fire. When done, dust them over with browned breadcrumbs, and dish them up very hot with a good glazed gravy made from veal. Garnish with slices of lemon.

SOFT CRABS BROILED.—After drying and cleaning them well season them highly with cayenne pepper and salt, and broil them over a clear hot fire. Serve very hot. Serve maître d'hôtel butter or sauce tartare with them.

SCALLOPED CHICKEN.—Cut cold roast or boiled chicken as for salad. Season it nicely with pepper, salt, minced onion and parsley. Moisten it with chicken gravy or cream sauce; fill scallop shells with the mixture and sprinkle bread-crumbs over the tops. Put two or three pieces of butter the size of a small white bean upon each, and brown them quickly in a hot oven.

CRAB CROQUETTES.—Pick the meat of boiled crabs and chop it fine. Season to taste with pepper, salt and curry-powder. Moisten it well with rich stock or cream, then stiffen it slightly with bread or cracker crumbs. Add two or three well-beaten eggs to bind the mixture. Form the croquettes, egg and bread-crumb them and fry them delicately in boiling lard. It is better to use a wire frying-basket for croquettes of all kinds.

SALLY LUNN.—Three eggs, one pint of sweet milk, salt, two tablespoonfuls of lard or butter (or one tablespoonful of each) melted, three pints of flour, half a pint of hop yeast. Separate the yolks and whites of the eggs and beat them very light. Add the milk to the yolks, then the salt and flour and whites. Stir in the yeast and beat all together until very light. Butter the cake or bread-pan, pour in the batter and let it rise over night. Bake an hour or longer in a moderate oven and serve it hot for breakfast.

BISCUIT GLACE.—Make a quart of rich boiled custard, flavor it with vanilla, and let it cool. Then mix with it a quart of grated pineapple or mashed peaches. Stir them well together and add enough sugar to allow for the loss in freezing. Freeze in the usual way, stirring in a pint of cream, whipped, when it is beginning to set in the freezer. Partly fill little paper cases with the mixture and smooth the tops nicely. Place them carefully in the cleaned and dried freezer and let them remain imbedded in ice for several hours. Sometimes the cases are filled with pistachio or chocolate ice-cream, in which case blanched almonds are laid over the tops when they are served. Or they may be filled with frozen whipped cream and served with a spoonful of some bright sherbert upon the top of each.

CREAM SPONGE CAKE.—Yolks of eight eggs beaten to the lightest possible cream, two cupfuls of sugar, three teaspoonfuls of baking-powder sifted well with flour. Bake in three jelly-cake pans. Make an icing of the whites of three eggs and one pound of sugar. Spread it between the cakes and sprinkle grated cocoanut thickly over each layer. It is delicious when properly made.

ICE-CREAM CAKE.—One pound of sugar, one pound of flour, half a pound of butter, whites of eight eggs, one teaspoonful of soda, two teaspoonfuls of cream of tartar, one tablespoonful of extract of almond, one-third of a cupful of sweet milk. Dissolve the soda in a tablespoonful of warm water. Bake in jelly-cake pans.

SPANISH CREAM.—One ounce of isinglass (the kind that comes in long pieces and is clear), one quart of milk, four eggs, sugar to taste. Dissolve the isinglass in the milk. Beat the yolks of the eggs to a cream with a little sugar, stir in the dissolved isinglass, taste to see if it is sweet enough, then stir it over the fire until it is just ready to come to a boil. Remove at once and flavor with vanilla or wine. Have the whites of the eggs beaten to a stiff froth, and stir them into the custard as soon as it is removed from the fire. They will remain partly on top. Pour the mixture into moulds and set in a cool place. In twenty-fours it will be ready to use. The top should look clear as amber and the custard should be below, forming two separate layers. It should be served with sauce.

FRIED CHICKEN.—Cut the chicken into six or eight pieces. Season well with salt and pepper. Dip in beaten egg and then in fine bread crumbs in which there is one teaspoonful of chopped parsley for every cupful of crumbs. Dip again in the egg and crumbs. Fry ten minutes in boiling fat. Cover the centre of a cold dish with Tartare sauce. Arrange the chicken on this and garnish with a border of pickled beets, or it can be served with cream sauce.

FILLET OF BEEF A L'ALLEMAND.—Trim the fillet and skewer it into good shape. Season well with pepper and salt. Have one egg and half a teaspoonful of sugar well-beaten together; roll the fillet in this and then in bread crumbs. Bake in the oven for thirty minutes. Serve with Allemand sauce poured around it.

STRAWBERRY CREAM.—Three pints of strawberries mashed fine. Strain the juice, and add a heaping cup of sugar, and then gelatine soaked and dissolved in a teacup of boiling water. Add a pint of whipped cream and pour into moulds.

GOLD CAKE.—One cup of sugar; half a cup of butter; two cups of flour; yolks of six eggs; grated rind and juice of a lemon or orange; half a teaspoonful of soda, mixed with the flour, and sifted twice. Cream the butter; add the sugar, then the beaten yolks and the flour, beating hard for several minutes. Last, add the lemon or orange juice, and bake; frosting, if liked.

CRULLERS.—One pint of sweet milk, one pint of sugar, quarter of a pound of butter, three or four eggs well beaten separately, two tablespoonfuls of cream of tartar, about two pounds of flour, or just enough to make a very soft dough, rose water and grated nutmeg to taste. Roll out thin; make the cakes small and round, with a hole in the centre. Fry in boiling lard, and after draining them well roll them in powdered sugar flavored with cinnamon. A little brandy may be added if liked.

NUT CANDY.—Three pounds of white sugar; half a pint of water; half a pint of vinegar; quarter of a pound of butter; one pound of hickory-nut kernels. Put the sugar, butter, vinegar and water together into a thick sauce-pan. When it begins to thicken add the nuts. To test it, take up a very small quantity as quickly as possible directly from the centre, taking care not to disturb it any more than is necessary. Drop it into cold water and remove from the fire the moment the little particles are brittle. Pour into buttered plates.

CANNED PINEAPPLE.—Pare ripe, juicy pineapples and cut them into slices an inch thick. Allow quarter of a pound of sugar to each pound of fruit. Put them into the preserving kettle together, and if there is not enough juice add very little water. As soon as they are well scalded through put into hot jars and seal at once.

LOBSTER SAUCE FOR BOILED FISH.—One small lobster, four tablespoonfuls of butter, two of flour, one-fifth of a teaspoonful of Cayenne, two tablespoonfuls of lemon juice, one pint of boiling water. Cut the meat into dice. Pound the "coral" with one tablespoonful of the butter. Rub the flour and the remainder of the butter to a smooth paste. Add the water, pounded "coral," and butter, and the seasoning. Simmer five minutes, and then strain on the lobster. Boil up once and serve.

HOUSEKEEPER'S POTATOES.—One quart of cold boiled potatoes, cut into dice; one pint of stock, one tablespoonful of chopped parsley, one of butter, one teaspoonful of lemon juice, salt, pepper. Season the potatoes with the salt and pepper, and add the stock. Cover, and simmer twelve minutes. Add lemon juice, butter, and parsley, and simmer two minutes longer.

CHICKEN SOUFFLE.—One pint of cooked chicken, finely chopped; one pint of cream sauce, four eggs, a little onion juice, salt, pepper. Stir the chicken and seasoning into the boiling sauce. Cook two minutes. Add the yolks of the eggs, well beaten, and set away to cool. When cold, add the whites, beaten to a stiff froth. Turn into a buttered dish, and bake half an hour. Serve with mushroom or cream sauce. This dish must be served the moment it is baked.

STRAWBERRY SPONGE.—One quart of strawberries, half a package of gelatine, one cupful and a half of water, one cupful of sugar, the juice of a lemon, the whites of four eggs. Soak the gelatine for two hours in half a cupful of the water. Mash the strawberries, and add half the sugar to them. Boil the remainder of the sugar and the water gently twenty minutes. Rub the strawberries through a sieve. Add the gelatine to the boiling syrup and take from the fire immediately; then add

the strawberries. Place in a pan of ice water and beat five minutes. And the whites of eggs and beat until the mixture begins to thicken. Pour in the moulds and set away to harden. Serve with sugar and cream. Raspberry and blackberry sponges are made in the same way.

MAIDS OF HONOR.—One cupful of sweet milk, one of sour, one of sugar, a lemon, the yolks of four eggs, a speck of salt. Put all the milk in the double boiler and cook until it curds; then strain. Rub the curd through a sieve. Beat the sugar and yolks of eggs together, and add the rind and juice of the lemon, and the curd. Line little patty pans with puff or chopped paste, rolled very thin. Put a large spoonful of the mixture in each one, and bake from fifteen to twenty minutes in a moderate oven. Do not remove from the pans until cold.

AMHERST PUDDING.—Three-fourths of a cupful of butter, three-fourths of a pint of sugar, four eggs, five tablespoonfuls of strained apple, the grated rind and the juice of a lemon, and nutmeg and rose-water, if you like. Bake half an hour in a moderate oven, in a shallow pudding dish that has been lined with a rich paste, rolled very thin. Let it become partially cool before serving.

COFFEE ICE CREAM.—This is a delicious dessert for hot weather. Pound two ounces of freshly roasted coffee in a mortar just enough to thoroughly crush the berries without reducing them to powder. Put them into a pint of milk with six ounces of loaf sugar; let it boil, then leave it to get cold; strain it on the yolks of six eggs in a double kettle, and stir on the fire until the custard thickens. Be sure that it does not curdle. When quite cold work into it a gill and a half of cream whipped to a froth. Freeze the mixture in the ice-cream freezer, then fill a plain mould with it and put it in the freezer till the time of serving.

MOUSSELINE PUDDING.—Four ounces of pounded sugar, four ounces of fresh butter, the rind of one lemon and the juice of two with the yolks of ten eggs, to be mixed together in a saucepan and stirred on a slow fire until quite hot; then strain the mixture into a basin and amalgamate lightly with it, as in making a soufflé, the whites of the eggs whisked into a stiff froth. Pour into a well-buttered mould, and steam for twenty minutes. Serve with any kind of jam sauce.

RAGOUT OF MUTTON.—Three pounds of any of the cheap parts of mutton, six tablespoonfuls of butter, three of flour, six button onions, or one of the common size, one large white turnip, cut into little cubes; salt, pepper, one quart of water and a bouquet of sweet herbs. Cut the meat in small pieces. Put three tablespoonfuls each of butter and flour in the stew-pan, and when hot and smooth add the meat. Stir until a rich brown, and then add water and set where it will simmer. Put three tablespoonfuls of butter in a frying-pan, and when hot put in the turnips and onions with a teaspoonful of flour. Stir all the time until a golden brown; then drain and put with the meat. Simmer for an hour and a half. Garnish with rice, toasted bread, plain boiled macaroni or mashed potatoes. Small cubes of potato can be added half an hour before dishing. Serve very hot.

COCOANUT ICE CREAM.—One quart of cream, one pint of milk, three eggs, one cupful and a half of sugar, one cupful of prepared cocoanut, the rind and juice of a lemon. Beat together the eggs and grated lemon rind, and put with the milk in the double boiler. Stir until the mixture begins to thicken. Add the cocoanu and put away to cool. When cool add the sugar, lemon juice and cream. Freeze.

RASPBERRY SHERBET.—Two quarts of raspberries, one cup of sugar, one pint and a half of water, the juice of a large lemon, one tablespoonful of gelatine. Mash the berries and sugar together and let them stand two hours. Soak the gelatine in cold water to cover. Add one pint of the water to the berries, and strain. Dissolve the gelatine in half a pint of boiling water, add this to the strained mixture and freeze.

OMELET SOUFFLE A LA CREME.—Four eggs, two tablespoonfuls of sugar, a speck of salt, half a teaspoonful of vanilla extract, one cupful of whipped cream. Beat the whites of the eggs to a stiff froth, and gradually beat the sugar and the flavor into them. When well beaten add the yolks, and lastly the whipped cream. Have a dish holding about one quart slightly buttered. Pour the mixture into this and bake just twelve minutes. Serve the moment it is taken from the oven.

BLACK CAKE.—Three cupfuls of butter, one quart of sugar, three pints of flour, half a pint of molasses, half a pint of brandy, half a pint of wine, one teaspoonful of saleratus, one ounce each of all kinds of spices, twelve eggs, three pounds of raisins, two of currants, half a pound of citron. Bake in deep pans, in a moderate oven, between three and four hours. This is one of the best of rich cakes.

DEVILLED CRABS.—One dozen fresh crabs boiled and pickled; quarter of a pound of fresh butter; one small teaspoonful of mustard powder; Cayenne pepper and salt to taste. Put the meat into a bowl and mix carefully with it an equal quantity of fine bread crumbs. Work the butter to a light cream, mix the mustard well with it, then stir in very carefully, a handful at a time, the mixed crabs and crumbs. Season to taste with Cayenne pepper and salt, fill the crab shells with the mixture, sprinkle bread crumbs over the tops, put three small pieces of butter upon the top of each, and brown them quickly in a hot oven. They will puff in baking and will be found very nice. Half the quantity can be made.

POTATO SCALLOPS.—Boil and mash the potatoes soft with a little milk or cream. Beat up hot with melted butter—a dessertspoonful for every half-pint of the potato—salt and pepper to taste. Fill some patty-pans or buttered scallop shells with the mixture, and brown in the oven when you have stamped a pattern upon the top of each. Glaze, while hot, with butter, and serve in the shells.

LADIES' CABBAGE.—Boil a firm white cabbage fifteen minutes, changing the water then for more from the boiling teakettle. When tender, drain, and set aside until perfectly cold. Chop fine, and add two beaten eggs, a tablespoonful of butter, pepper, salt, three tablespoonfuls rich milk or cream. Stir all well together, and bake in a buttered pudding dish until brown. Serve very hot.

GINGER CRACKERS.—One pound of brown sugar, one pound of butter, four pounds of flour, one quart of molasses, two ounces of ground ginger, two ounces of ground cloves. Put half the flour into a large bowl, and rub the butter into it with the hands until it becomes as fine as pulverized sugar; then add the sugar, molasses and spices. Work in gradually the rest of the flour and knead it as thoroughly as for bread. The more it is kneaded the crisper and better the crackers will be. Roll out thin, cut with a round cake-cutter, and bake in a moderately heated oven. These crackers are excellent, and will keep fresh and crisp for a long time if excluded from the air.

FROZEN PUDDING.—Boil one quart of milk and stir into it a full teaspoonful of arrowroot, moistened with milk. When smooth, pour it over the well-beaten yolks of six eggs, stirring hard. Add strawberry preserves, brandied fruits, fruit cake or plain cake, citron, stoned raisins, and currants. Sweeten to taste, add half a tumblerful of sherry wine and one and a half wineglassfuls of brandy. Flavor with vanilla and freeze as ice-cream. Mould in a melon-shaped mould. After turning the pudding out upon a platter, spread all over it the whites of six eggs beaten to a stiff froth with a little sugar and brandy.

CHOCOLATE JELLY.—Four small cakes of chocolate grated and one and a half pints of milk boiled together. Then add sugar and vanilla to taste, and one box of gelatine dissolved in a little water. Boil all together for a few minutes, then set away to cool.

BANANA FRITTERS.—Four eggs, one pint milk, a little salt, flour enough to make a light batter. Beat the eggs into the milk, and add salt and flour. Stir in, pretty thickly, bananas, sliced thin. Fry in hot lard.

ROSE PERFUME.—Gather all the fragrant roses you can—no matter if you are a week gathering,—and when you get a good many, take an iron mortar and pestle, like a druggist has, fill the mortar and pound the leaves to a pulp. It will be quite like a lump of dough. Then take your thimble and use it for a measure—fill it full of the mixture, empty out into your hand, and between your palms roll and roll, until you make a compact little ball, round as a marble. Make up all your rose dough material this way, place on plates and dry in the sunshine. They will be dark and brown-looking, but

"The scent of the roses will cling to them still."

These are to put in drawers and trunks **and**

bandboxes, and among your bed and table and towel linen, and they will be just as fragrant for years as when you plucked the short-lived beauties and buried your face lovingly down into their glowing red hearts. I have made beads of them by making them a trifle smaller and drying them with pins stuck through the centres. Then they can be strung. Again, I have made them into little thin cakes the size of crackers. They are nice any way, for the great charm remains the same. Now supposing an old blind man didn't die and will you his tin box and a'l his traps, including an apothecary's mortar and pestle, like he did me. Not likely. But "where there's a will," etc., etc. You can take your stew kettle and your potato-masher in a punch.— [Weekly Hawkeye.

HOMINY CROQUETTES.—To a cupful of cold boiled hominy, add a tablespoonful of melted butter; stir well, then add gradually a cupful of milk, stirring and mashing the hominy until it becomes a soft, smooth paste. Then add a teaspoonful of white sugar and a well-beaten egg. Roll into oval balls with floured hands, roll in beaten eggs, then in bread crumbs, and fry in boiling lard.

SALMON PATTIES.—Cut cold cooked salmon into dice. Heat about a pint of the dice in half a pint of cream, or Hollandaise sauce. Season to taste with Cayenne pepper and salt. Fill the shells and serve. Cold cooked fish of any kind may be made into patties in this way. Use any fish sauce you choose —all are equally good.

SHIRRED EGGS.—Butter a dish, and break into a number of eggs, taking care that they do not encroach upon each other enough to break the yolks. Sprinkle pepper and salt over them, put a small piece of butter upon each, and add a tablespoonful of cream for each egg. Bake in a hot oven until the whites are set.

NUN'S TOAST.—Cut four or five hard-boiled eggs into slices. Put a piece of butter half the size of an egg into a saucepan, and when it begins to bubble add a finely chopped onion. Let the onion cook a little without taking color, then stir in a teaspoonful of flour. Add a cupful of milk, and stir until it becomes smooth; then put in the slices of eggs and let them get hot. Pour it over neatly trimmed slices of hot buttered toast. The sauce must be seasoned to taste with pepper and salt.

CORN LOAF.—Four eggs, whites and yolks beaten as light as possible, separately; one quart of corn meal; quarter of a pound of butter; two quarts of boiling milk; a teaspoonful of salt mixed well with the corn meal. Melt the butter in the milk, and scald the corn meal with it, beating and stirring well until it becomes perfectly smooth, then add the light yolks and lastly the stiffly beaten whites. Bake in a quick oven. Half the quantity will make a good sized loaf.

TRANSPARENT PUDDING.—Butter a pudding dish, and line it with slices of stale sponge cake cut an inch thick. Put stewed or ripe fresh fruit, or preserves, in the bottom of the dish upon the cake.

Beat to a cream the yolks of eight eggs, quarter of a pound of sugar and half a pound of butter. Flavor to taste with rose or peach water, add half a grated nutmeg, and stir in lightly the stiffly beaten whites of the eggs. Pour the mixture over the fruit and bake half an hour. Beat the whites of four eggs to a stiff froth and add four tablespoonfuls of sugar; spread over the pudding after it is baked and return it to the oven for a few minutes to color. To be eaten cold, with or without cream.

TIP-TOP CAKE.—One pound of sugar, one cupful of butter, four eggs, one cupful of milk, one pound of chopped raisins, half a pound of chopped figs, half a grated nutmeg, one small teaspoonful of soda, one teaspoonful of cream of tartar, flour to make it of a proper consistency.

POTATOES A LA NEIGE.—Boil or bake the potatoes, mash them well, dress them with cream, butter and salt, and press them through a colander into the hot dish in which they are to be served. Pile them up high and serve very hot.

SPINACH.—Wash and pick over carefully a peck of young and freshly gathered spinach. It is better to wash it in several waters, and then, that it may be entirely free from grit or sand, throw it finally into fresh, clear water. Drain it well by shaking it in a sieve. Boil it about fifteen or twenty minutes, in slightly salted boiling water. When tender, drain it well, shaking it about in a colander until quite dry. Serve it on pieces of toast, dipped for a moment in the water the spinach was boiled in. Season with pepper and salt and put plenty of butter, cut into small pieces, over it. Garnish the dish with slices of hard-boiled eggs.

MACARONI A L'ITALIENNE.—Cut a chicken into joints and stew or fry it. In either case make a cream gravy. Boil a large handful of macaroni in salted boiling water until it begins to swell, then pour off the water. After pouring off the water, cover the macaroni with milk. Season nicely with pepper and salt and throw in a large onion, peeled. Let it boil until tender, then drain it well. Arrange the chicken in the centre of a hot platter, and make a border around it of the macaroni; pour the cream gravy over all, and serve at once.

SWEET-BREAD CROQUETTES.—A plump tongue, boiled until tender, then cooled, seven or eight sweet-breads. Scald the sweet-breads, remove the sinews, then fry them in butter. Chop the tongue very fine, then pound it to a smooth paste in a mortar. Pound the sweet-breads to a paste and add it to the tongue. Mix well together and season to taste with pepper, salt, grated onion and minced parsley. Add three well-beaten eggs, and moisten the whole with veal stock, making it as moist as it can be handled. Form the croquettes, egg and bread crumb them, and let them color a golden brown in boiling lard. If allowed to take too deep a color they will harden and be spoiled. Sometimes the mixture is made quite moist with veal stock and then stiffened slightly with bread crumbs.

LUCIA PUDDING.—One large cocoanut grated and the milk; eight large Irish potatoes, boiled and mashed smooth; three pints of milk; one nutmeg: one gill of rum or brandy; a lump of butter the size of an egg; one pound and a quarter of sugar; six eggs. Take the whites of the eggs and half the sugar, whip them up well and put on the top of the pudding after it is done, returning it then to the oven to brown. Bake about two hours.

HUCKLEBERRY PUDDING.—One quart of ripe fresh huckleberries or blueberries; half a teaspoonful of mace or nutmeg; three eggs well beaten, separately; two cupfuls of sugar; four large teaspoonfuls of butter; one cupful of sweet milk; one pint of flour, two teaspoonfuls of baking powder. Roll the berries well in the flour, and add them last of all. Bake half an hour and serve with sauce. There is no more delicate and delicious pudding than this.

WOODCOCK, FRIED—Dress and wipe them clean. Tie the legs close to the body; skin the heads and necks, and tie the beaks under the wing; tie, also, a very thin piece of bacon around the breast of each bird, and fry in boiling lard. It only requires a few moments—say two minutes—to cook them. Season, and serve them on toast.

POIVRADE SAUCE.—Mince an onion; fry it a yellow color, with butter in a stew-pan; pour on a gill of vinegar; let it remain on the fire until a third of it is boiled away; then add a pint of gravy or stock, a bunch of parsley, two or three cloves, pepper and salt; let it boil a minute; thicken it with a little flour and butter; strain it and remove any particles of fat.

STUFFING FOR VEAL.—Soak half a pound of bread (with the crust off in tepid water, then squeeze it dry. Put three ounces of butter into a stew-pan, and when hot stir in a small onion minced (one and a half ounces), which color slightly; then add the bread, with three tablespoonfuls of parsley (half an ounce) chopped fine, half a teaspoonful of powdered thyme, a little grated nutmeg, pepper, salt and a gill of stock. Stir it over the fire until it leaves the bottom and sides; then mix in two eggs.

FRITTERS.—Four eggs; one pint of milk; the rind of one grated lemon; a little salt; flour to make a light batter. Beat the eggs into the milk; add lemon, salt and flour. Fry in hot lard and serve with wine.

PRESERVED TOMATOES.—Take ripe, but not soft, little yellow tomatoes and pour boiling water over them to take off the skins. Make a syrup of one pound of sugar to one of tomatoes, putting in only enough water to dissolve the sugar. Take three lemons to each seven pounds of tomatoes; slice, and put in the syrup, first removing the seeds. When the syrup is boiled clear put in the tomatoes and boil gently three-quarters of an hour.

PEACH SHORTCAKE.—Make a soft dough of one quart of sifted flour mixed with two heaping tea spoonfuls of baking powder, a generous tablespoonful of butter, a little salt, and sufficient sweet milk. Roll out thin, put a layer in a baking-pan, and sprinkle with flour and bits of butter; make four layers like this, using no butter and flour on the top layer. Bake in a quick oven, turn out upside down, remove the layers, and place ripe peaches, cut up and sweetened, between each layer. Serve as a cake, with cream and sugar.

FILLET OF BEEF.—After it is trimmed and larded, put it into a small baking-pan, in the bottom of which are some chopped pieces of pork and beef-suet; sprinkle some salt and pepper over it and put a large ladleful of hot stock into the bottom of the pan, or it may be simply basted with boiling water. Half an hour (if the oven is very hot, as it should be,) before dinner put it into the oven. Baste it often, supplying a little hot stock if necessary.

POULET A LA MARENGO.—Cut up an uncooked fowl as for a fricassee, and fry the pieces in olive oil, with a bruised clove of garlic, pepper, salt and a fagot of sweet herbs. Take three table-spoonfuls of the oil used in frying the fowl, add some minced mushrooms, a little shallot and parsley also finely minced, a glass of white wine, as much stock, free from fat, as you want sauce, pepper and salt to taste. Let the sauce boil a few minutes; dish up the pieces of fowl, pour the sauce over, and serve.

GREEN CORN SOUP.—Cut the kernels from a dozen large ears of green corn, and just cover them in a stewpan with boiling water. Boil half an hour, add a quart of milk, pepper and salt to taste, and a spoonful of fresh butter. Beat three eggs very light with a tablespoonful of corn-starch. When the soup just comes to the boiling point again stir in the eggs, and serve quickly.

STRING BEANS IN SALAD.—String the beans and boil them whole; when boiled tender and they have become cold, slice them lengthwise, cutting each bean into four long slices; place them neatly, the slices all lying in one direction, upon a platter. Season them, an hour or two before serving, with a marinade of pepper, salt, and three spoonfuls of vinegar to one spoonful of oil. Just before serving drain from them any drops that may have collected, and carefully mix them with a French dressing. This makes a delicious salad.

GERMAN CAKE.—One pound of flour, three-quarters of a pound of butter, six ounces of sugar, one egg, half a cupful of rum. Bake in a pie-pan, pressing the cake until it is about one-quarter of an inch high. Before baking sprinkle sugar and ground cinnamon on top; after it is baked, cut it into squares while it is yet warm.

CROQUANTE CAKE.—Three-quarters of a pound of shelled almonds, half a pound of citron, three-quarters of a pound of sugar, three-quarters of a pound of flour, six eggs. Blanche and halve the almonds, and slice the citron; mix them well together and roll them in flour; add to them the sugar, then the eggs (well beaten), lastly the flour. Butter shallow pans and lay in the mixture two inches thick. After it is baked in a quick oven, slice the cake into strips one inch wide, and turn every strip. Return the pan to the oven and bake the sides a little. When cold, put it away in tin boxes. This cake will keep a year or more, and for reserve use is quite invaluable.

BEEFSTEAK, WITH OLIVES.—Take a piece of rump steak, cut it in slices three-eighths of an inch thick, and trim them into shape. Melt plenty of butter in a baking-tin, lay the fillets of beef in this, and let them stand in a warm place for an hour or so; then sprinkle them with pepper and salt, and fry them in some very hot butter, turning them to let both sides take color. Stone a quantity of olives and parboil them. Fry some onions a brown color in butter, add a little flour, and, when that is colored, as much stock as you want sauce, with pepper, salt, and spices to taste. Let the sauce boil, then strain it, add the olives, and serve when quite hot, with the fillets in a circle round them.

VEAL HASH.—Take a teacup of boiling water in a sauce-pan, stir in an even teaspoonful flour wet in a tablespoonful cold water, and let it boil five minutes; add one half-teaspoonful black pepper, as much salt, and two tablespoonfuls butter, and let it keep hot, but not boil. Chop the veal fine, and mix with it half as much stale bread crumbs. Put it in a pan and pour the gravy over it, then let it simmer ten minutes. Serve this on buttered toast.

SALAD.—Put in the bottom of the salad dish a layer of cold boiled potatoes, sliced thin; sprinkle pepper and salt over the slices, then put a layer of boiled lima beans, and so on, alternately, until the dish is full. Season each layer with pepper and salt, and over the top, a few minutes before serving, pour enough vinegar to flavor the salad; mix oil with the vinegar; mustard may be added to suit the taste.

MEAT PIE.—Cut cold cooked meat into quite small dice, add pepper, salt, a little nutmeg, and two or three sprigs of chopped parsley; also a little thyme and a piece of bay-leaf if you have them, but the two latter herbs may be omitted. Put a little butter into a saucepan, and when hot throw in a tablespoonful of flour, which brown carefully; pour in then several tablespoonfuls of hot water, or better, stock; mix well; then introduce the meat dice; stir all well over the fire, cooking it thoroughly. Just before taking it up, mix in one or two eggs. It should be quite moist, yet consistent. Put a thin pie-crust into a pudding-dish. Fill in a few table-spoonfuls of the mixture; then lay on it a thin strip of bacon; continue these layers until the dish is filled. Now fit a piece of crust over the top; turn the edges in a fancy manner, and make a cut in the centre. Take a strip of pie-paste, form it into a tie or knot, wet the bottom, and place it over the cut in the centre of the pie, so as not to obstruct the opening.

LEMON JELLY.—Half a box of gelatine soaked in half a pint of water; juice of five large lemons; two cupfuls of loaf-sugar, or sugar to taste; beaten white and shell of an egg; one and a half pints of boiling water. Soak the gelatine in the half pint of water half an hour. Rub several of the pieces of the sugar on the peel of the lemon, to soak the oil on the surface. Pour a pint and a half of boiling water on the soaked gelatine, and add lemon juice, sugar and egg; let it come to a boil, then set it at the side of the range a few moments; skim carefully and pass through the jelly-bag into moulds.

STEWED TOMATOES.—Pour boiling water over six or eight large tomatoes to remove the skin, and then cut them into a saucepan. When they begin to boil pour away a little of the juice; add a small piece of butter, pepper, salt, and a very little sugar. Let them cook for about fifteen minutes, stirring in well the seasoning. Some add a few bread or cracker crumbs.

SAUCE A L'INDIENNE (FOR FISH).—Make half a pint of white sauce, add a tablespoonful of curry powder, and some pickles chopped small, with a little of the vinegar.

BOSTON BAKED BEANS.—Pick over the beans, rejecting all imperfect ones; soak them over night; in the morning parboil them till the skins crack open, dip them from the kettle with a perforated skimmer into a glazed earthen pot, salt to taste. Put in the top of the pot a piece of fat salt pork with the rind scored, cover with water, put on a cover of dough or tin and bake in an oven not very hot, for six hours. If the oven is of brick they may be put in at night and remain till morning. Butter or suet may be used instead of pork. Sometimes a tablespoonful of molasses is put in when the salt is added.

RIZ A LA TURQUE.—Put into a saucepan six cupfuls of stock or broth in which you have previously dissolved a good allowance either of tomato paste, French tomato sauce, or the pulp of fresh tomatoes passed through a sieve, pepper and salt to taste. When it boils throw in, for every cupful of stock, half a cupful of fine rice well washed, and dried before the fire. Let the whole remain on the fire until the rice has absorbed all the stock, then melt a large tablespoonful of butter, and pour it over the rice. At the time of serving, and not before, stir lightly to separate the grains, but do this off the fire.

MACARONI A L'ITALIENNE.—Cut into small, thin pieces two pounds of fresh, lean beef, slice a small onion, chop and then pound in a mortar quarter of a pound of fat bacon; fry the bacon and onion together, then add the beef and turn all frequently. When the beef becomes slightly colored, turn the whole contents of the frying-pan into a hot saucepan. Add a pint of boiling water, boil up for one minute, skim thoroughly, and sprinkle in a salt-spoonful of salt and a little pepper, then simmer gently for two hours, skimming occasionally. Strain this gravy through a hair sieve, and when cold take off the fat. When ready to use make the gravy hot and mix with the fourth part of it a tablespoonful of tomato sauce; then add by degrees the rest of the gravy, stir over a slow, clear fire and boil three minutes. Put in boiling salted water a half pound of Naples macaroni; boil quickly twenty to twenty-five minutes, drain in a colander, which shake before the fire a minute or two to make the macaroni perfectly dry. Put the macaroni on a hot dish, mixing through it two or three tablespoonfuls of grated Parmesan cheese, pour the hot gravy over it, mixing well; and serve with a dish of grated Parmesan. This is an excellent dish with which to begin dinner on days too hot for smoking a up. The proportions may of course be varied to suit the number of persons served.

PICKLED GRAPES.—Take ripe grapes; remove imperfect and broken ones. Line an earthen jar with grape leaves; then fill with grapes. To two quarts of vinegar allow one pint of white sugar, half an ounce of ground cinnamon, and a quarter of an ounce of cloves. Let the vinegar and spices boil for five minutes; then add the sugar. Let it come to a boil and when cold pour over the grapes. If poured on while hot it shrivels them, even if it does not break the skin and spoil the appearance of the pickles.

VEAL CUTLETS A LA MILANAISE.—Trim some veal cutlets into a uniform shape, and dip them in liquefied butter—that is, butter melted on the runge. Then pass them through a mixture of equal parts of bread crumbs and grated Parmesan cheese, properly peppered and salted. When set dip them in a beaten-up egg and pass them through the mixture again, then fry them brown. Boil a small quantity of macaroni, dress it with butter, Parmesan cheese and tomato sauce with the yolk of an egg stirred into it. Place the macaroni on a dish and the cutlets in a circle round it.

MAITRE D'HOTEL SAUCE.—Melt a couple of ounces of butter in a saucepan, mix thoroughly with it two tablespoonfuls of flour, add half a pint of hot water, white pepper and salt to taste, and stir until it thickens: it too thick add more hot water. Mince very finely a handful of parsley, knead it with half an ounce of butter, add this to the sauce with the juice of half a lemon, stir it well on the fire and serve.

TO CAN PEACHES.—Cling stones are best. Pare, halve, and stone them. Boil the stones or pits until all the flavor is extracted; then pour off the water from the pits, and when it is at the boiling-point, throw into it enough peaches to fill three or four cans; sprinkle over sugar to taste, or about as much as would be sprinkled over fresh peaches for the table. When just scalded, can them, placing round pieces of writing paper dipped in brandy over the tops of the peaches before putting on the covers.

TIMBALE DE SPAGHETTI.—Break some spaghetti into very short lengths and boil it thoroughly. Drain it before the fire and add to it plenty of fresh butter or a cup of strong, rich gravy; then mix with it one or two beaten eggs, according to quantity. When the macaroni is nearly cold, fill with it a plain mould which had been previously buttered and sprinkled with fine bread crumbs. Press the macaroni well down, leaving a hollow in the centre, in this place a well flavored mince of lamb, poultry, or game; fill up the mold with more macaroni,

pressing it down compactly. Bake in a moderately quiet oven, turn out and serve very hot.

RIPE CUCUMBER PICKLES. — Pare and seed ripe cucumbers. Slice each cucumber lengthwise into four pieces, or cut it into fancy shapes as preferred. Let them stand twenty-four hours covered with cold vinegar. Drain them; then put them into fresh vinegar, with two pounds of sugar and one ounce of cassia buds to one quart of vinegar. Boil all together twenty minutes. Cover them closely in a jar.

MINUTE PUDDING.—One quart of milk, salt, two eggs, about a pint of flour. Beat the eggs well; add the flour and enough milk to make it smooth. Butter the saucepan, and put in the remainder of the milk well salted; when it boils stir in the flour, eggs, etc., lightly, let it cook well. It should be of the consistency of thick corn mush. Serve immediately with the following simple sauce, viz.: Milk sweetened to taste and flavored with grated nutmeg.

CALVE'S BRAINS.—Soak the brains in water till all the blood is removed, dry them in a clean cloth and then fry in butter or oil. Garnish with parsley and erve. Or, after soaking them, boil them in milk for twenty minutes, then drain them from the milk and put them in vinegar for three or four hours.

SPINACH A LA CRÈME.—Pick over and wash the spinach, and cut the leaves from the stalks. Boil in hot water, a little salted, about twenty minutes. Drain, put into a wooden tray or upon a board; chop very fine, and rub through a colander. Put into a saucepan; stir until it begins to smoke throughout. Add two tablespoonfuls of butter for a good-sized dish, a teaspoonful of white sugar, three tablespoonfuls of milk, salt and pepper to taste. Beat, as it heats, with a silver fork or wire spoon. Flavor with a little nutmeg. Cook this until it begins to bubble up as you beat it. Pour into a deep dish, surround with sliced egg, and serve.

CUCUMBER TOAST.—Peel fresh crisp cucumbers of medium size; cut lengthwise into slices, place in cold water for a few minutes; drain, and dip each slice into flour; then fry quickly, until of a light brown color, in butter or beef drippings. Place the slice of buttered cucumber hot from the pan between slices of buttered toast and serve at once. The cucumbers may be seasoned with pepper and salt, and a little mustard may be added when taken from the pan.

INDIAN FRITTERS.—Put three tablespoonfuls of flour into a basin, and pour over it sufficient boiling water to make it into a stiff paste, taking care to stir and beat it well, to prevent its getting lumpy. Leave it a little time to cool, and then break into it —without beating them first—the yolks of four eggs and the whites of two, and stir and beat all well together. Have ready some boiling lard or clarified dripping. Drop a dessertspoonful of batter in at a time, and fry the fritters of a light brown. They ought to rise so much as to be almost like balls.

Serve them on a hot dish, with a spoonful of jam or marmalade dropped in between each tritter.

CHERRY PUDDING.—Two eggs, one cupful of sweet milk, three teaspoonfuls of yeast powder, flour to make a stiff batter, as many cherrres or fruit of any kind as can be stirred in. Boil or steam it two hours. Serve with fruit sauce of the same kind of fruit of which the pudding is made.

BAKED BERRY ROLLS.—Roll biscuit dough thin, in the form of a large square or into small squares. Spread over with berries. Roll the crust, and put the rolls into a dripping-pan close together until full; then put into the pan water, sugar and pieces of butter. Bake them. Serve with any of the pudding sauces.

RANAQUE BUNS.—One pound of butter, one and a quarter pounds of sugar, two pounds of flour, six eggs, four tablespoonfuls of ground cinnamon. Mix the cinnamon with the flour; rub the butter to a cream, then mix the flour with it. Beat the sugar with the eggs, then altogether as little as possible. Distribute this by the spoonful into rough-looking cakes on buttered tins placed at a little distance apart. This is a very nice lunch-cake.

CUCUMBER A LA CREME.—Peel and cut into slices (lengthwise) some fine cucumbers. Boil them until soft, salt to taste, and serve with delicate cream sance.

SOUP OF STRING-BEANS.—Make a strong stock as follows: Add to a knuckle of veal three quarts of water, a generous slice of salt pork, and two or three slices of onion. Let it simmer for five hours, then pour it through a sieve or colander into a jar. It is better to make this stock the day before it is served, as then every particle of fat may be easily scraped off the jelly. Ten minutes before dinner put into a saucepan two ounces of butter, and when it bubbles sprinkle in four ounces of flour; let it cook without taking color; then add a cupful of hot cream, a pint of the heated stock, and about a pint of green string-bean pulp, i. e., string-beans boiled tender with a little pork, then pressed through a colander and freed from juice. After mixing all together, do not let the soup boil, or it will curdle and spoil. Stir it constantly while it is on the fire. Just before it is sent to table, sprinkle over the top a handful of little fried fritter beans. They are made by dropping drops of fritter batter into boiling lard. They will resemble navy-beans, and give a very pleasant flavor and appearance to the soup. If this pretty addition be considered too much trouble, little dice of fried bread may be added instead. The soup should be rather thick and served quite hot.

FRICANDEAU OF VEAL.—What is called a fricandeau of veal is simply a cushion of veal trimmed into shape, larded and braised. Cut a thick slice (three or four pounds) from a fillet of veal, trim it, and lard it on top. Put some pieces of pork into a braising-kettle, or saucepan if you have no braising-kettle; also slices of carrot, an onion with cl ves stuck in, a stick of celery, and some parsley.

Put in the meat, sprinkle over pepper and salt, and cover it with well-buttered paper. Now fill the pan with boiling stock, or water enough to just cover the meat. Put on a tight lid. If it is a braising-pan, set it upon the fire, with live coals on top. If a common saucepan, cover it, and put it into a hot oven. It will take about two hours, or two hours and a half, to cook it.

TAPIOCA CREAM.—Soak a teacupful of tapioca over night in milk. The next day stir into it the yolks of three eggs well beaten, and a cupful of sugar. Place a quart of milk on the fire; let it come to the boiling point, and then stir in the tapioca, and let the whole cook until it has thickened; then take it off the fire and stir in the whites of the eggs beaten to a froth. Flavor to taste. A small portion of the beaten whites of the eggs can be saved to decorate the top. Stir into the latter a little sugar, put it into a paper funnel, press it out over the top of the pudding according to fancy, and place it in the oven a few moments to color.

ENGLISH POUND-CAKE.—One pound of butter beaten to a cream; one pound of pounded sugar; ten eggs (whites and yolks beaten separately); one pound of dried flour; eight ounces of almonds; eight ounces of candied peel; two wineglasses of brandy. When all are well beaten together, add three pounds of English currants and one pound of raisins, both dredged in flour. Set it immediately in a moderate oven, and bake three hours at least.

CREAM OF RICE SOUP.—Two quarts of chicken stock (the water in which fowls have been boiled will answer); one teacupful of rice; a quart of cream or milk; a small onion; a stalk of celery; salt and pepper to taste. Wash rice carefully, and add to chicken stock, onion and celery. Cook slowly two hours (it should hardly bubble). Put through a sieve; add seasoning and the milk or cream, which has been allowed to come just to a boil. If milk, use also a tablespoonful of butter.

STEWED STEAK WITH OYSTERS.—Two pounds of rump steak, one pint of oysters, one tablespoonful of lemon juice, three of butter, one of flour, salt, pepper, one cupful of water. Wash the oysters in the water and drain into a stewpan. Put this liquor on to heat. As soon as it comes to a boil, skim and set back. Put the butter in a fryingpan, and when hot, put in a steak. Cook ten minutes. Take up the steak, and stir the flour into the butter remaining in the pan. Stir until a dark brown. Add the oyster liquor and boil one minute. Season with salt and pepper. Put back the steak, cover the pan, and simmer half an hour; then add the oysters and lemon juice. Boil one minute. Serve on a hot dish with points of toast for a garnish.

CHICKEN CROQUETTES.—One solid pint of finely chopped cooked chicken; one tablespoonful of salt; half a teaspoonful of pepper; one cupful of cream or chicken stock; one tablespoonful of flour; four eggs; one teaspoonful of onion juice; one tablespoonful of lemon juice; one pint of crumbs; three tablespoonfuls of butter. Put the cream or stuck on to boil. Mix the flour and butter together, and stir into the boiling cream; then add the chicken and seasoning. Boil for two minutes; then add two of the eggs, well beaten. Take from the fire immediately and set away to cool. When cold, shape and fry. Many people think a teaspoonful of chopped parsley an improvement.

LEMON SPONGE.—The juice of four lemons, four eggs, one cupful of sugar, half a package of gelatine, one generous pint of cold water. Soak the gelatine two hours in half a cupful of the water. Squeeze the lemons, and strain the juice on the sugar. Beat the yolks of the eggs and mix them with the remainder of the water. Add the sugar and lemon to this, and cook in the double boiler until it begins to thicken; then add the gelatine. Strain this mixture into a tin basin, which place in a pan of ice water. Beat with the whisk occasionally, until it has cooled, but not hardened. Now add the unbeaten whites of the eggs, and beat all the time until the mixture begins to thicken. Let it thicken almost to the point where it cannot be poured, and then turn into a mould and set away to harden. Remember that the whites of the eggs must be added as soon as the mixture cools, which should be in about six or eight minutes, and that the mixture must be beaten until it begins to harden. The hardening is rapid after it once begins, so that it will be necessary to have the moulds all ready. The sponge will not be smooth and delicate if not poured into the moulds. If for any reason you should get the mixture too hard before pouring, place the basin in another of hot water, and let the sponge melt a little; then beat it up again. Serve with powdered sugar and cream.

BISQUES.—Bisques may be made with shell-fish, such as lobsters, crabs, prawns, etc.; also of snipes or quails; rabbits, too, are used in this way. *Crabs:* Pick the white meat from the claws of a large boiled crab, and lay it between two plates in a cool place until required. Pound the white meat as well as the pulpy part found in the shell, with about half the quantity of well-boiled rice—the rice must have been boiled in stock, not in water—to this add a quart of good stock; warm it, and rub it through a tammy to set aside in a basin till wanted. Just before dinner-time set the purée in a stewpan on the fire to get hot, but on no account to boil, or it would curdle; keep stirring with a wooden spoon. The meat from the claws should in the meantime have been shredded, warmed in a little stock, and put into the soup-tureen. Finish by adding to the soup a pint of boiling cream and a little cayenne pepper; stir together, and pour over the shredded meat and serve. *Lobster:* Take the pithy part, the coral, and the spawn from two hen lobsters. Pound a small quantity of the coral and spawn in a mortar, with a piece of butter the size of a walnut and an anchovy; add a very little cayenne, rub it through a sieve, and keep it in a cool place till wanted, as well as the rest of the coral, etc. Cut the meat into small pieces, and fry it in a little butter, with a carrot and a head of

celery, cut into very small pieces; add to this a sprig of thyme, a blade of mace, and a very little pepper and salt; fry this for about five minutes, taking care that it does not burn, and, if necessary, moistening it with a little white Rhenish wine, of which about a pint will be required. Add any of the wine that may not have been used during the frying to the stewpan, into which the mixture must now be transferred; let it boil quickly for twenty minutes, stirring it during the time. Then drain the lobster on a sieve, and pound it thoroughly in a mortar, putting it back again into the stewpan with the spawn, coral, etc., which was reserved, and also with the liquor in which it was boiled; add to it a pint and a half of good white stock, then rub the purée through a tammy into a basin, and let it remain until wanted. A quarter of an hour before serving, put it into a stewpan on the fire, stirring it all the time, and being very careful not to let it boil, or it might curdle. Stir in a small piece of light-colored glaze, and season it with a very little cayenne and the juice of half a lemon; the lobster butter made from the coral must also now be added. Have in the tureen two or three dozen tails of prawns and about the same number of small quenelles or balls made of whiting; pour the purée over them, and the bisque is then ready for table.

CHEESE SOUP.—One and a half cupfuls of flour, one pint of rich cream, four tablespoonfuls of butter, four of grated Parmesan cheese, a speck of cayenne, two eggs, three quarts of clear soup stock. Mix flour, cream, butter, cheese and pepper together. Place the basin in another of hot water and stir until the mixture becomes a smooth, firm paste. Break into it the two eggs and mix quickly and thoroughly. Cook two minutes longer and set away to cool. When cold, roll into little balls about the size of an American walnut. When the balls are all formed, drop them into boiling water and cook gently five minutes; then put them into the soup tureen and pour the boiling stock on them. Pass a plate of finely grated Parmesan cheese with the soup.

BROILED LOBSTER.—Split the meat of the tail and claws, and season well with salt and pepper. Cover with soft butter and dredge with flour. Place in the broiler, and cook over a bright fire until a delicate brown. Arrange on a hot dish, pour Bechamel sauce around, and serve.

POTTED PIGEONS.—Clean and wash one dozen pigeons. Stand them on their necks in a deep earthen or porcelain pot, and turn on them a pint of vinegar. Cut three large onions in twelve pieces, and place a piece on each pigeon. Cover the pot and let it stand all night. In the morning take out the pigeons and throw away the onions and vinegar. Fry, in a deep stewpan, six slices of fat pork, and when brown, take them up, and in the fat put six onions sliced fine. On these put the pigeons, having first trussed them, and dredge well with salt, pepper and flour. Cover, and cook slowly for forty-five minutes, stirring occasionally; then add two quarts of boiling water and simmer gently two hours. Mix four heaping tablespoonfuls of flour with a cupful of cold water, and stir in with the pigeons. Taste to see if there is enough seasoning, and if there is not, add more. Cook half an hour longer. Serve with a garnish of rice or riced potatoes. More or less onion can be used ; and if you like it so, spice the gravy slightly.

BREAKFAST VEAL.—Butter a small oval dish very thoroughly, and fill with bits of cold stewed veal seasoned with pepper, salt and a little nutmeg; put in alternately with layers of cracker crumbs, moisten with gravy, put bits of butter over the top, and bake. When it is brown turn out of the dish on a hot platter, and garnish with parsley. If it is not too moist it will keep its form when it is turned out.

CHICKEN PUREE.—Pick into small bits cold roast or broiled chicken, and season it with salt and pepper. Boil the bones and skin in enough water to cover them, strain and return to the fire. When it boils stir in for one cupful of the stock one small teaspoonful of butter. Add a little celery salt and stir in the meat. Serve with triangles of bread which have been fried crisp in very hot lard.

ORANGE PUDDING.—One pint of milk; the juice of six oranges and the rind of three; eight eggs; half a cupful of butter; one large cupful of granulated sugar; a quarter of a cupful of powdered sugar; one tablespoonful of ground rice; paste to line the pudding dish. Mix the ground rice with a little of the cold milk. Put the remainder of the milk in the double boiler, and when it boils stir in the mixed rice. Stir for five minutes; then add the butter, and set away to cool. Beat together the sugar, the yolks of eight eggs and whites of four. Grate the rind and squeeze the juice of the oranges into this. Stir all into the cooked mixture. Have a pudding dish holding about three quarts lined with paste. Pour the preparation into this, and bake in a moderate oven for forty minutes. Beat the remaining four whites of the eggs to a stiff froth, and gradually beat in the powdered sugar. Cover the pudding with this. Return to the oven and cook ten minutes, leaving the door open. Set away to cool. It must be ice cold when served.

PLAIN SPONGE CAKE.—Beat the yolks of four eggs together with two cups of granulated sugar. Stir in gradually one cup of sifted flour and the whites of four eggs beaten to a stiff froth, then a cup of sifted flour in which two teaspoonfuls of baking-powder has been stirred, and lastly, a scant teacup of boiling water stirred in a little at a time. Flavor, add salt, and however thin the mixture may seem, do not add any more flour. Bake in shallow tins.

CHICKEN CREAM (*Crème de Volaille.*)—Pound the white flesh of a fowl into a pulp, pass it through a horsehair seive, put it back into the mortar, and work into it the yolks of three or four eggs and a gill of cream; flavor with pepper, salt, and grated nutmeg, and, if liked, a suspicion of shallot. When the mixture is perfectly amalgamated, butter a plain mould, arrange thin slices of truffles at the bottom and sides of it by pressing them on the butter, then put in the mixture, which should only half fill the mould. Tie a piece of paper on the top, place the mould into a saucepan half filled with hot water, and steam it for an hour and a half. Serve with truffle sauce. Truffles may be omitted altogether, and the dish served with tomato sauce.

TAPIOCA CREAM SOUP.—One quart of white stock ; one pint of cream or milk ; one onion ; two stalks of celery; one-third of a cupful of tapioca; two cupfuls of cold water; one tablespoonful of butter; a small piece of mace; salt, pepper. Wash the tapioca and soak over night in cold water. Cook it and the stock together very gently for one hour. Cut the onion and celery into small pieces, and put on to cook for twenty minutes with the milk and mace. Strain on the tapioca and stock. Season with salt and pepper, add butter, and serve.

RISSOLES OF CHICKEN.—Mince very finely some remnants of chicken freed from skin, etc.; add an equal quantity of ham or tongue and a little chopped parsley. Heat in a saucepan with a good-sized piece of butter mixed with a large pinch of flour; add white pepper, salt and nutmeg to taste; moisten with a little stock or hot water; then stir in, off the fire, one or two yolks of eggs beaten up, with a squeeze of lemon, and lay the mixture on a plate to get cool. Make a paste with some flour, a little water, two eggs, a pinch of salt, and two or three of sugar; roll it out to the thickness of a penny piece, stamp it out in round pieces three inches in diameter; put a piece of the above mince on each, then fold it up, fasten the edges by moistening them with water, and trim them neatly with a fluted cutter. Dip each rissole in a beaten-up egg, and fry a nice color in hot lard ; serve with fried parsley.

FISH IN WHITE SAUCE.—Flake up cold boiled halibut and set the plate into the steamer, that the fish may heat without drying. Boil the bones and skin of the fish with a slice of onion and a *very* small piece of red pepper; a bit of this the size of a kernel of coffee will make the sauce quite as hot as most persons like it. Boil this stock down to half a pint; thicken with one teaspoonful of butter and one teaspoonful of flour, mixed together. Add one drop of extract of almond. Pour this sauce over your halibut and stick bits of parsley over it.

BEEF CROQUETTES.—One cup of lean beef; half a cup of the fat; half a cup of cold boiled or fried ham; a piece of onion as large as a silver dollar; one teaspoonful of salt; half a teaspoonful of pepper; a pinch of sage, and a little grated lemon-peel. Chop all as fine as possible, or put through a mincing machine. Heat, with half a cup of stock or cold soup, and add one egg well beaten ; form into croquettes; roll in egg and bread crumbs, and fry in boiling lard.

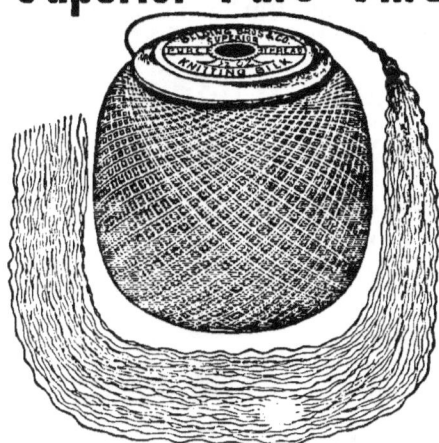 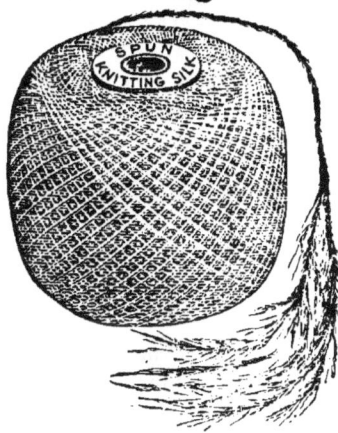

USE

CLARK'S
TRADE
O.N.T.
MARK
SPOOL COTTON.

ON WHITE SPOOLS.

IT IS THE BEST FOR HAND AND MACHINE SEWING.

ALSO,

CLARK'S
BEST CROCHET COTTON,

MADE FROM SEA ISLAND COTTON.

Marshall's Spool Linen Thread.

GEORGE A. CLARK, Sole Agent.

SOLD EVERYWHERE.

NEW-YORK TRIBUNE PUBLICATIONS.

SPECIAL ISSUES.

I. THE TRIBUNE ALMANAC FOR 1884.

Price 30 cents. Five copies for a Dollar.
Edited by Edward McPherson.

The TRIBUNE ALMANAC for 1884 contains the most carefully prepared and trustworthy figures and tables of returns of the late State Elections, and of other important elections, which returns, it is well known, are always consulted with marked interest in political campaigns, and will be especially during the Presidential Election of this year. The TRIBUNE ALMANAC is admittedly the Standard Book of Reference,—without a rival,—in matters of this nature, and will consequently be inquired for and sought after extensively by politicians, writers, and voters generally throughout the country. The Almanac also contains twenty pages, this year, of the highest interest and value relating to THE NEW TARIFF. In parallel columns are given the present rate of duty, the former rate, and the one recommended by the Tariff Commission: the value of each kind of goods imported, and the duty collected. The Almanac gives in simple form the substance of elaborate tables and a long and verbose law. In view of the continued agitation of the tariff, the Almanac will be in great demand the coming year. The Almanac also contains a wide variety of condensed information about Governmental affairs, the public laws, etc.

II. THE TRIBUNE INDEX.

A complete Key to the World's History during 1883, with a Table of Topical Heads. Price, 50 cents. The TRIBUNE INDEX for 1875, 1876, 1877, 1878, 1879, 1880, 1881, 1882, and 1883. Price, 50 cents each.

PUBLICATIONS FOR SALE.

The following works are offered for sale to TRIBUNE readers at the prices named:

Young's Bible Concordance, 1,100 pages, 4to, cloth binding, by mail, postage prepaid.................... $2 00
"Recollections of a Busy Life," by Horace Greeley; 624 pages, sheep covers, postage prepaid............... 3 00
"What I Know of Farming," by Horace Greeley, 335 pages, cloth covers, postage prepaid............... 1 50
"The Library of Universal Knowledge"; 15 vols. of 960 pages each, cloth; per set (special binding, extra)... 12 00
"The New-York Tribune;" a Sketch of Its History; Illustrated; 24 pages, paper cover..................... 10
Representative American Journalists; 13 heads of managers of leading papers, 22x28 inches........... 50
Portrait of General Garfield; engraved, 22x28 inches.. 10
Portrait of Mrs. Garfield; a companion of the above.. 10

TRIBUNE EXTRAS.

No. 44.—The Cipher Dispatches. The Florida, South Carolina and Oregon secret telegrams, with the keys that translate them. In folded sheet form, 5 cents. In pamphlet form, 40 pages, large type, 25 cents.

No. 46.—The Prophetic Conference. Verbatim reports of the different addresses and papers. Octavo, 120 pages. 25 cents.

No. 59.—Woman's Extra. Practical directions for Fancy Work, Patterns, Knitting and Crochet. 10 cents.

No. 62.—Knitting and Crochet. 48 pages. 20 cents

No. 64.—Sunday Dinners. A Manual of Home Cookery. In pamphlet form. 25 cents.

No. 76.—Stocking Knitting. A Manual of Household Industry. Pamphlet form. Price, 10 cents.

No. 77.—The New-York Tribune, jr. Stories for Those Least Little People. A handsome little book of 56 pages, with colored borders. Price, 10 cents.

No. 82.—New Patterns in Knitting and Crochet. With illustrations. Pamphlet, 72 pages. Price, 25 cents.

No. 83.—Astronomy. Six Lectures by Prof. Young. Sheet form. Price, 10 cents.

TRIBUNE NOVELS.

The cheapest and best series of fiction.

Every Novel is complete and unabridged; would cost from seven to ten times as much as The Tribune Novel. Price, 10 cents each, unless otherwise noted. Sent, post-paid, on receipt of the price.

1. LORDS AND LADIES. Published by arrangement with A. K. Loring, Boston.

*4. THE WOOING O'T. By Mrs. Alexander. Double Number, price, 20 cents.

*5. FAR FROM THE MADDING CROWD. By Thomas Hardy. Double Number, price, 20 cents.

6. GOOD LUCK. By E. Werner. Translated from the German for THE TRIBUNE.

17. ALICE LORRAINE. By R. D. Blackmore. Double Number, price, 20 cents.

18. THE CURATE IN CHARGE. By Mrs. Oliphant.

9. OLYMPIA. A Romance. By R. E. Francillon.

10. BLACK SPIRITS AND WHITE. By Frances Eleanor Trollope.

11. TWO LILLIES. By Julia Kavanagh.

12A CHARMING FELLOW. By Frances Eleanor Trollope.

13. DRIFTED BY THE SEA. By Henry Whitney Cleveland.

14. CHERRY RIPE. By Helen B. Mather, author of "Comin' Thro' the Rye."

18. THREE WIVES. By the author of Lords and Ladies. 36 pages, price 20 cents.

20. DISMISSED. A Novel. By William Osborn Stoddard.
21. THE SHADOW OF A SIN. A fascinating short story of love and adventure.

22. THE REBEL OF THE FAMILY. A novel of absorbing interest.

23. LEFT IN TRUST. A Novel. The Story of a Lady and Her Lover; 32 pages, Weekly Tribune size. Price 10 cents.

24. LIESCHEN. A Tale of an Old Castle. Translated for THE TRIBUNE. Price 10 cents.

25. DOROTHY. A Story of Waiting. Price 10 cents.

26. PROPER PRIDE. A Story of Life in India and in England. "The best novel in twelve years." Price 10 cents.

* Published by arrangement with Henry Holt & Co., whose Leisure Hours Series includes authorized editions of all Mr. Hardy's and Mrs. Alexander's works.

† Published by arrangement with Harper Brothers, whose Library of Select Novels includes authorized editions of Mr. Blackmore's and Mrs. Oliphant's works.

THE TRIBUNE,
NEW-YORK.

New-York Tribune.

THE LEADING PAPER.

HEARTILY REPUBLICAN IN POLITICS.

Devoted to American Manufacturing and Farming and American Homes.

THE STANDARD AUTHORITY.

THE TRIBUNE will be sent, postage paid, to mail subscribers in all parts of the United States at following reduced rates:

	1 Year.	6 Months.	3 Months.	1 Month.
DAILY, with Sunday	$8 50	$4 25	$2 15	$0 75
DAILY, without Sunday	7 00	3 50	1 75	0 75
SUNDAY TRIBUNE	1 50	....	....	....

SEMI-WEEKLY, $2 50 a year; in clubs of ten, $2 a year, with extra copy to man sending club.

WEEKLY, $1 25 a year; in clubs of ten, $1 a year, with extra copy to man sending club.

Counting postage, about two cents a copy on all editions. The most, in quantity and value, for the least money, of any paper in America.

THE TRIBUNE this year is cheaper than ever, and better than ever. It has not reduced character with price. A trusted, clean, wholesome family paper, it has long enjoyed the largest circulation among the best people—the industrious, frugal and moral, whom every community recognizes as its best citizens—and it means to keep and increase this circulation by continuing to deserve it.

THE TRIBUNE is the leading New-York paper—complete in news, strong and sound in comment, pure in tone, large and legible in print—spending money lavishly for news, and as lavishly for brains to handle it. It is recognized as the authority on political, business, bank, railroad, and financial, literary, educational, scientific, social and religious intelligence.

THE TRIBUNE is heartily Republican, and believes that the restoration of the Democratic party to power, after twenty-four years' exile, would be as disastrous as a revolution. Every important material interest in the country dreads such a change in 1884. THE TRIBUNE confidently believe it can be prevented, and to that end asks your aid.

THE TRIBUNE is always on the side of morality, good order, reform and progress. It warmly sympathizes with every practical effort to restrict the traffic in intoxicating liquors. It always favors the cause of honest labor; and in the interest of the American Workingman supports a Protective Tariff. It has no interest for or against corporations, to hinder its taking the just and fair course, best for all the people and the whole country. It is the organ of no person or faction, is under no control save that of its Editor, and knows no obligation save that to the public.

THE WEEKLY TRIBUNE has been for a third of a century **the favorite of our substantial rural population.** It has a larger and wider circulation than any other weekly issued from the office of a daily in the United States. A complete weekly newspaper of sixteen, and sometimes twenty or twenty-four pages, its agricultural matter is believed by farmers to be the best published. It contains full markets and many features of interest in the home circle. This year two series of special articles will be printed, one for young men, the other for farmers.

THE SEMI-WEEKLY TRIBUNE is the best substitute for the Daily. It has all the matter of the latter of more than transient interest, and all the special features of the Weekly. Sixteen to twenty pages.

THE TRIBUNE will be indispensable during the Presidential canvass.

The following books are offered as premiums with the WEEKLY and SEMI-WEEKLY: "The Indexed Atlas of the World," 904 pages, 125 maps and charts, 225 colored diagrams, and 650 pages of description; "Wood's Household Practice of Medicine," 2 vols., 819 and 942 pages, illustrated—a valuable work; Ridpath's entertaining illustrated "History of the United States," 752 pages; "The Sonatas of Beethoven;" Webster's and Worcester's Unabridged Dictionaries, latest editions.

THE TRIBUNE makes an offer for the formation of Town Libraries. Send for circular.

AGENTS WANTED AT EVERY POST-OFFICE.

Circulars describing fully all TRIBUNE premiums, and sample copies, sent free on application.

www.ingramcontent.com/pod-product-compliance
Lightning Source LLC
Chambersburg PA
CBHW032140080426
42733CB00008B/1149